the BUSINESS *of* COACHING WITH HORSES

Advance Praise

"Witty, well-written, creative, and informative, this book offers sound, practical advice for finding your niche and overcoming obstacles to success. Schelli's unique process is relevant to anyone in the business of working with horses to help people excel in life."

—**Linda Kohanov**, author of *The Tao of Equus,
Riding Between the Worlds, The Way of the Horse,
Power of the Herd* and *The Five Roles of the Master Herder.*

"This is a wonderfully insightful and surprisingly fun resource! A must read for setting your equine assisted adventure off on the correct lead!"

—**Chris Irwin**, author of *Dancing with
Your Dark Horse* and *Horses Don't Lie*

"*The Business of Coaching with Horses* made me laugh and cry in turn. It also hit me at a deep, soul level, exactly where it was needed. After many years of struggling to make my beloved equine facilitated practice function as a viable business, this book has given me more than just clues as to where I need to re-focus my energy and attention. With a unique blend of spiritual alchemy and practical steps, Schelli's book is a joy to read, providing the reader with a great set of tools to really help you do the essential work of running an equine facilitated business. This book is long overdue and a must read for all working in this field. It will add an essential component for those committed to developing their business in a way that is fulfilling, and yes, financially rewarding too. Thank you, Schelli. from the bottom of my heart; you're a genius!"

—**Angela Dunning**, author of *The Horse Leads the Way: Honoring
the True Role of the Horse in Equine Facilitated Practice.*

"Schelli Whitehouse delivers an interactive learning experience woven into her courageous and transparent story. She is naming an issue for the industry of coaching with horses that has been sorely lacking for years. I see this book as a huge contribution to the folks who are committed to becoming serious business owners. I especially appreciate that she offers wisdom from the pioneers in this industry, it was fun to read the words of my dear friends and fellow travelers. She captured our unique take on the world and our work. Her succinct and engaging style will help others to find their niche and help to make a positive impact through coaching and horses."

—**June Gunter**, author of *TeachingHorse: Rediscovering Leadership*

"In her book, *The Business of Coaching with Horses*, Schelli Whitehouse carefully crafts a step-by-step guide and delivery system for what it takes to become successful in the field of equine assisted education. Distinct from a collection of stories and good ideas, this is a teaching book designed for coaches to tackle real challenges (like your relationship to money), and discernment between working *in your business* and working *on your business*. This book is truly a treasure trove of effective practices and deep wisdom all in one place, destined to hone your passion and your purpose in realizing ambitions, dreams, and goals. This book is a must read (and a must do) for anyone who is in the business of coaching with the help of horses."

—**Alyssa Aubrey**, HorseDream© USA,
author of *The Road to Success* with Jack Canfield

Very funny, very readable, very helpful. Schelli has written a book that will make a difference with some of the key "soft" skills and self-knowledge any practitioner in the field should be fluent in: your relationship with money and the impact on self-worth, pricing your services, what you are great at (and not so great at), and many more important conversations you need to have with yourself as you step into this work. If you want to do Equine Assisted Anything, you'll need to be able to articulate answers to her questions in this easy-to-read, bite-size segments of important, content. Super well-done, Schelli!

—**Shannon Knapp**, Horse Sense of the Carolinas, Inc.,
author of *Horse Sense Business Sense, Vol 1* and
More than a Mirror: Horses, Healing and Therapeutic Practice

"There are certain non-negotiables in the process of creating financial success and abundance in life. Schelli Whitehouse has been invaluable in supporting me and Equine Alchemy over the years. Save yourself time, effort, and money by following her advice about 'How to Reach More Clients, Feed Your Horses, and Change the World!' But beware: as in Equine Alchemy, transformation is not an option! Abundance comes in many forms."

—**Lisa Murrell**, founder of Equine
Alchemy Coach and Facilitation Training

"*The Business of Coaching with Horses* gives you all you need to get your mindset in the state of success. Schelli's enthusiasm carries through in each chapter as she guides you through the framework you need to set up the foundation of your practice and take care of any old 'money stuff.' I would recommend this book for any person starting an equine business."

—**Kathy Pike**, founder of the Academy for Coaching with Horses

"Like most things, 'horse assisted therapy' can be done to a high standard or it can be one more way to exploit the good nature of captive horses. Anyone can set themselves up as a 'professional' horse trainer or offer programs that include horses. In *The Business of Coaching with Horses*, Schelli Whitehouse outlines the educational experiences, personal qualities, and business acumen a person needs to establish a valid program that supports the needs of its clients. I enjoyed the many quotes Schelli used to accentuate her ideas. Each chapter is supported by specific exercises that motivate readers to look closely at themselves and the fine points involved with creating a service of value to other people. Schelli's book will guide people to the 'high standard' end of the continuum of quality equine assisted programs. The comments from practitioners of successful programs, at the end of the book, are illuminating."

—**Hertha James**, author of *Conversations with Horses, An In-Depth Look at Signals and Cues Between Horses and Their Handlers*

"Schelli Whitehouse is a beacon for visionary game changers: those who honor the soul of the horse, care deeply about transforming lives, and possess the determination and pioneering spirit to develop and run a business that creates a new paradigm here on Earth. Whew- no small task! Success in this unique entrepreneurship arena demands nothing less than equal amounts of compassion, brass tacks practicality and perseverance, and an ongoing commitment to personal growth and healing. As she admits: "Your crap is going to come up too. Especially if you've never run a successful business before, and you are now the leader of your own company. You must let it out, and keep a muck bucket nearby."

Her own story is a testimony to the power of breaking through the limiting beliefs about money, self-definition and self-worth that plague most of us, and result in dwindling bank accounts and failed businesses. She lovingly pays it forward with anecdotes and action steps, attitudes, 'Quantum Leap' principles, workbook exercises and plenty of advice from highly regarded industry experts. Schelli's tools empower the reader to get crystal clear about themselves, create a solid foundation for their relationship with money and realize that their beliefs, wants and actions must be in alignment in order to bring in clients and generate income.

The horses are already doing their miraculous work to help us heal. They are simply waiting for us to step into our power to meet them halfway. This book is a must-have primer for those who want to truly partner with the horse to fulfill a mutual, higher purpose and still pay their bills."

—**Sandra Mendelson**, author, *We Walk Beside You: Animal Messages for an Awakening World*

"Spoken with the soulful introspection of a deeply reflective journeyer in the realm of evolutionary coaching, Schelli Whitehouse delivers a vulnerable and equally provocative perspective on the do's and don'ts of aligned thinking within a successful equine practice.
She generously shares her wisdom with the eager neophyte in an uncanny way certain to entertain, educate and most of all INSPIRE!"

—**Dr. Tatiana H. Irvin**, author of *The Reluctant Intuitive* and *Prosperity Through the Development of Emotional Intuition*

"Do the work! Schelli makes it easy for you. She's giving you the keys to the kingdom of a successful equine assisted coaching business. Now it's up to you to put it into practice."

—**Kami Guildner**, author of *Firedancer: Your Spiral Journey to a Life of Passion and Purpose*

"Schelli's concept of a "spiritual entrepreneur" and the rigorous journey it takes to get there is a beautiful description for all who follow the Way of the Horse. She takes people step by step through a process which helps identify "Who they are, what they do and whom they are here to serve". Each individual can re-discover and claim what I call "the blueprint of the soul". Schelli's words, "active striving for the fulfillment of the soul's work", clearly state what it takes to integrate your essence with your expertise. Many people embarking on this work in equine facilitated learning or psychotherapy come to this calling as a second career. *The Business of Coaching with Horses* helps people with encouragement and support to make the calling a sustainable practice for themselves and the horses. I highly recommend this book and it will be a requirement for my mentorship students."

—**Kathleen Barry Ingram**, MA, founder of T
he Sacred Place of Possibility

the BUSINESS *of*
COACHING
WITH
HORSES

How to Reach More Clients,
Feed Your Horses, and Change the World

SCHELLI WHITEHOUSE

NEW YORK

LONDON • NASHVILLE • MELBOURNE • VANCOUVER

the BUSINESS of COACHING WITH HORSES
How to Reach More Clients, Feed Your Horses, and Change the World

Published in New York, New York, by Morgan James Publishing in partnership with Difference Press. Morgan James is a trademark of Morgan James, LLC. www.MorganJamesPublishing.com

The Morgan James Speakers Group can bring authors to your live event. For more information or to book an event visit The Morgan James Speakers Group at www.TheMorganJamesSpeakersGroup.com.

ISBN 978-1-68350-993-6 paperback
ISBN 978-1-68350-994-3 eBook
Library of Congress Control Number: 2018934771

Cover Design by:
Rachel Lopez
www.r2cdesign.com

Interior Design by:
Bonnie Bushman
The Whole Caboodle Graphic Design

Photo for front and back cover by:
Nicole Waite

In an effort to support local communities, raise awareness and funds, Morgan James Publishing donates a percentage of all book sales for the life of each book to Habitat for Humanity Peninsula and Greater Williamsburg.

Get involved today! Visit
www.MorganJamesBuilds.com

To Joe Whitehouse,
the traveling companion of a lifetime.
And to Anna and Grayson,
with love from your *woo-woo* Mom ~ xo

TABLE OF CONTENTS

INTRODUCTION

For You — Dear Horse & Soul Practitioner,
Your passion and your hunger for self-expression moves me. I see your expertise is wrapped in love and compassion for the seeker of excellence; the seeker of peace; the seeker of self-worth. Your gifts and talents for healing and transformation deserve to be acknowledged! I am in awe of your willingness to sacrifice your time, your heart, and your soul to helping others heal from the pains of their past. To the people who come to you, you give, not only hope for their future, you give them the tools to transform a mere existence of coping with what is into creating their hearts' desire. You give them the gift of their own wings.

And here is something else I know about you and your endeavor into horse and soul entrepreneurship: You gotta eat too!

Please do not starve to death because you're either not making enough money to live on (by giving yourself away), or you are a best kept secret, and nobody (or hardly anyone) can find you! Your good work is worthy of support and acknowledgement. Don't let it fade away.

Stop straddling the fence between your perceptions of failure and success. It is time to wholeheartedly jump into your higher calling. Take the leap ... the net will appear.

This book is for you, my soulful fence-sitter, to be used as a tool, (and a kick in the pants) for bringing your healing, creativity, and transformative coaching with horses to people who need you and will happily pay you for your extraordinary talent and service.

Regardless of your story, your education, or the balance of your bank account, it only takes one quantum leap to access the next highest version of the grandest vision you have ever had for yourself. All while doing good for others along the way.

The world needs you now.

Ready ... Set ... Leap!

Chapter One

THE BIRTH OF AN EQUINE INSPIRED ENTREPRENEUR

*You have to grow from the inside out. None
can teach you, none can make you spiritual.
There is no other teacher but your own soul.*
—Swami Vivekananda

My Story

If there were a twelve-step program for personal development junkies,
I'd be a card-carrying member.

For a long time, I was a closet spiritual junkie, hiding under the
covers and reading the courageous words of so many others. I kept my
habit mostly hidden because I could never identify the result that I

was sure was going to occur within myself after completing each new program, training, or "do-it-yourself" transformation manual. I never seemed to get to that place where I could put down the book or walk out of the classroom and proclaim to the world, "Look at me! I am enlightened: I'm whole, happy, healthy, pain-free, and I can make a million dollars in 90 days—watch me!"

After the initial high of the "ahas" that I gleaned from each new training, the disappointment of the "new me" still not being able to sustain my lofty goals began to gnaw away at my psyche. I didn't understand why these techniques, philosophies, and writing exercises didn't stick for me. Oh, it all made perfect sense intellectually, but I wasn't living it. Why wasn't I getting where I wanted to go?

From an outsider's perspective, my life was perfect. The stuff was all there. I had a nice house, a wonderful husband, a girl, a boy, a dog, a cat, a fish, and a horse (we had a bird but the cat ate him). We had awesome friends and family. We loved to travel, cook, entertain, and spend too much on the holidays. I was living the American Dream, and I was still not satisfied. Yet, I felt hollow inside and was racked with guilt because of it.

What Was Wrong with Me?

> *The world sometimes feels like an insane asylum. You can decide*
> *whether you want to be an inmate or pick up your visitor's badge.*
> **—Deepak Chopra**

Part of my depression was a symptom of not knowing what I wanted to be when I grew up. I was very busy taking care of my family. In 27 years of marriage, the longest we have ever lived in one house is five years. Due to my husband's career, we moved six times between 2000 and 2007. At that time, my primary function was to pack a house, sell a house, buy a house, unpack a house, research schools, get the kids settled in, and then, just as I would begin to feel like part of a community and find a niche for myself, the cycle would begin again. I was good at it, but I was also exhausted and resentful and beginning to wonder, "What's the point?"

During the summer of 2007 we moved from Colorado, where we all loved living, back to Raleigh, North Carolina where we had left in 2000. Once again, I started going through the motions of taking care of stuff and feeling invisible, with no identity of my own. Like the photographer's blank piece of photo paper, I felt I needed to be soaked in the proper developer solution before I could see the details of the image of who I really was. Those images are developed in a darkroom. No one sees them except the person developing the images. In my mind, I developed hundreds of images of myself. I would look into the mirror and stare into the eyes of a woman I didn't know, a reflection of myself, begging her to help me be somebody I wasn't already.

Figured It Out!

A sensible man will remember that the eyes may be confused in two ways: by a change from light to darkness, or from darkness to light. And he will recognize that the same thing happens to the Soul.
—**Plato**

Around this time, the movie *The Secret* hit the mainstream. I was already familiar with most of the presenters featured. I watched that film with tears running down my face, thinking, *Schelli, you know all of this stuff, yet why aren't you happy, healthy, wealthy, whole, and complete?*

As hokey and one-dimensional as the movie was, I am grateful for its timing in my life. I'm not sure what it was about that little film, versus the many books I had read over the years, but it prompted me to start paying attention to what I wanted to have happen for myself, and not only to the needs of everyone else.

Jack Canfield was in the movie, and I bought *The Success Principles: How to Get from Where You Are to Where You Want to Be!* That book became my bible, it helped me save my marriage and maybe even my life. That's quite a testimonial, I know. But, this is why I believe it was different: the book is experiential. There are 64 principles of success in his book, and most of them require action! The most significant success principle for me at the time was a "life purpose" exercise that helped me to reveal and articulate my own core values and reconnect with choices that made me feel happy and fulfilled. I began to get curious again about possibilities in my life.

In the process of completing the 'life purpose' exercise, it revealed that my work needed to have something to do with horses and something to do with personal development. *Right,* I thought. *What am I supposed to do with that?* At the time, I had never heard of life coaching and the only professions I was aware of with horses were riding instructors, horse trainers, and handicap therapy, none of which I had any desire to pursue. I threw the book across the room.

The Way of the Horse

A higher source of wisdom taps wellsprings of inspiration and energy, connecting you more deeply to your soul's purpose. To engage with this powerful archetype, you must be willing to ask for help and embody the wisdom and power of the horse.
—**Linda Kohanov**, *The Way of the Horse*

Shortly after I threw Jack Canfield's *64 Principles* across the room, a second book came into my life, *The Tao of Equus* by Linda Kohanov. I know this book may have had a significant impact on you as well. If you haven't read it, I insist you order it immediately! As a practitioner of equine assisted learning and healing, not reading this book would be like becoming a Doctor of Philosophy and never reading the works of Plato. Impossible!

I was fascinated and moved by the stories and insights she shared with regards to humans relating to horses in a powerful, energetic way that I hadn't known existed. I became intensely interested in what Linda Kohanov was up to in the world. I read the books she had referenced in her text and along the way discovered other equine assisted learning programs that were beginning to sprout up around the country as well as something called life coaching.

At the time, there were psychotherapeutic and physical therapy programs that incorporated horses, and there were purely facilitated learning programs, but there were no actual coach training programs with horses.

Shortly after we got settled in Raleigh, I went through the Equine Assisted Growth and Learning Associations (EAGALA) certification training and though I learned a lot, I was hungry for more. I decided to make the significant investment and commitment to sign up for Linda Kohanov's Eponaquest apprenticeship program. As fate would have it, when I got to her website I saw a new training being offered. *Coach Training Through the Way of the Horse*, taught by Lisa Murrell and Linda Kohanov. I couldn't sign up fast enough!

Today, I can't imagine learning to embody the art of coaching in any other way.

The Birth of an Equine Inspired Entrepreneur

Whether you're an entrepreneur, an employee, a student, a homemaker, a writer, it's time to start forgetting about all the ways the world has promised you safety and comfort.
—James Altucher

Have you ever been facilitating an experience or held sacred space for someone else and found yourself witnessing your own experience at the same time? You are still present, yet a part of you is jumping up and down for joy, celebrating your purpose! That happened for me in January of 2009. I hosted my first equine assisted workshop with friends and some friends of friends. I titled it, "The Next Highest Version of You!" During the first day of the workshop I was explaining to the group what I meant by the phrase, "The Next Highest Version of You". I adopted it from the book, *Conversations with God* by Neale Donald Walsh. In the book, God explains that our purpose is to continually experience the next highest version of the grandest vision you have ever had for yourself. While sharing this with the group I was having my own out-of-body experience as I witnessed myself doing the work I was passionately in love with and had only dreamed was possible. I was at that moment, living the next highest version of myself and who I was becoming.

After the many years of inhaling the wisdom of the "masters," I was finally beginning to exhale. The work with the horses taught me to embody the wisdom in a way that was more than knowledge swirling around in my brain, it was now integrated into the next highest version of me. I felt like I was bestowed with new superpowers, and it was time to get to work saving the world!

Horse Transformation for Hire!

I opted for a freelance writing career.
I was lucky enough to have the means to do it.
—**Matt Ridley**

Outside of some part-time network marketing experience from another lifetime, I had no formal business skills. I never went to business school and had no marketing or public relations training at all. I had no idea how to invite people to be a client. I did however, seem to have a knack for creating workshops and hosted a couple of those before I realized how much work it was going to take to make any money with this endeavor. I loved what I was doing, but I could barely afford to take care of my horse at the rate I was going.

Do you remember the Peanut's cartoons where Lucy sets up her booth with the sign on the front that says, *Psychiatric Help 5¢*? Then she sits and waits for clients to come and pay her 5¢ in exchange for her wisdom (which of course, was terrible). Well, my wisdom may not have been so terrible, but my marketing strategy was, and it was equally ineffective!

Six months after my first workshop, I felt dead in the water. I began looking for marketing training and found a "Money, Marketing and Soul Coach Certification" program being taught by Kendall Summerhawk in Tucson, AZ. During that year I developed my own programs and incorporated horses into the retreat experience.

I learned the value of what I had to offer and how to help others discover their own value. I became an expert at creating program offers and designing coaching packages, all while not having a clue on how to run a business.

By all outward appearances I was a huge a success. Behind the scenes a perfect storm was gathering strength and I couldn't outrun it, not even on horseback.

Goals Without Soul

> *It's a common misconception that money is every entrepreneur's*
> *metric for success. It's not, and nor should it be.*
> —**Richard Branson**

I've re-invented myself many times throughout this lifetime. My PhD from the "School of Hard Knocks" instilled a sense of gratitude, empathy, and understanding for the struggle of others. I thought I no longer needed "healing," therapy, or alcohol to overcome the history of my broken home, family mental illness, being on my own since age 17, a horrendous car accident, a brief marriage to a drug dealer, and numerous other "frog kissings" in search of the one true prince. I've survived rape, abortion, robbery at gunpoint, childbirth, cancer, and betrayal, but nothing prepared me for the devastation I experienced as I watched my whole identity disintegrate into oblivion, erased from existence. I was a walking bag of contradictions. I had worked every minute of every day to become a six-figure coach, and I thought that it was a done deal. It was done alright. No deal.

I had become obsessed with earning $100K my first year because I wanted to be a six-figure coach with "horse power." At 12 months, I had earned just under $80K. I didn't break $100K until the 18th month of launching my business. Still pretty good, right? I was making more money than ever before in my life, and at the same time, I was crushed that I hadn't hit my goal within the 12-month mark. On top of that I had $20,000 of credit card debt. I forgot to celebrate the "Soul" part of my purpose and was caught up in the "goal" of wanting to establish my self-worth and credibility.

As if on cue, new clients stopped enrolling in my programs, and many of the clients I had were going through their own personal struggles due to the recession. Some couldn't finish paying for their programs. I had not managed the "business" aspect of my business at all. I felt like such a fraud that I refunded the few clients I had and stopped marketing for more than two years!

Permission to Be Seen

> *Our greatest weakness lies in giving up. The most certain*
> *way to succeed is always to try just one more time.*
> **—Thomas A. Edison**

I chose to share these specific moments of my life with you because they were the last few twists and turns on a roller-coaster of life that I believed I had no control over. The twists and turns; highs and lows you have encountered have led you to this moment, reading these words. You may be at a significant choice point in your work and life: a point where you are ready to fully commit to your profession of making a difference for humans and horses.

I'm writing this book for you, dear kindred spirit. You are the soulful entrepreneur that deserves to be seen. I know the power of your work. I want you to succeed and create a sustainable practice for you and your herd, because your work is changing the world. I believe that with every fiber of my being.

It took me years to reconcile my beliefs around money and my identity. I don't want it to take that long for you. We have to sift through what is valid, what is conditioned, what is made up, and what is the truth. This is what it is all about. We are here to discover the truth for ourselves at each moment of our development and to celebrate every small success (or setback) with the same gratitude as the big ones. It's time to give ourselves permission to make mistakes and to change our minds, permission to be a professional, and permission to be seen.

Chapter Two

A LITTLE HORSE SENSE FOR HUMANS

*My mission it to help equine-inspired transformation become the
most sought-after personal development alternative available.
As popular as Yoga and Starbucks!*
—**Schelli Whitehouse**

A Little Horse Sense for Humans

The past ten years of being an equine assisted entrepreneur has been
the most rigorous personal and spiritual development classroom I
never knew I wanted (often didn't want). The trial and error, or I
should say the trial and "terror" of growing my own business led
me to the biggest "Aha" of my life! And that is what this book is
about. Whether you have been an entrepreneur for some time or

are just getting started, I want you to understand that your work is vitally important. You are being called to a higher purpose for a critically important reason with regards to the conscious evolution of our planet.

When I first began writing this book, I wanted to call it *One Quantum Leap*, because I know by the time you reach the end of this book you'll be prepared to leap into the next highest version of the grandest vision you've ever had for your equine assisted practice. Once the framework is in place and you push the GO button, you will be transported to another version of yourself, the version that is successful with transforming the lives of others through coaching and horses. When that happens, your life will feel as if you took a quantum leap out of this moment and into an exponentially different, more expanded version of yourself and your work.

This book is for you if you are a professional equine assisted practitioner, or someone who is ready to breathe some new life into your practice, who needs to reach more clients, feed your horses (and yourself), and wishes to have your life and work live in harmony. The lessons and tools are designed to prepare you to present yourself as the go-to person in your own unique area of expertise while creating a balanced and abundant business for you and the horses you work with!

Are You Ready to Make the Leap?

> *Doing is a quantum leap from imagining.*
> —**Barbara Sher**

Quantum leaps rarely happen out of the blue. They result from the active striving for the fulfillment of your Soul's work. There is more than one pathway to achieve a quantum leap. Actually, there are many pathways to be developed. They are called neural pathways. Neural pathways literally change your body's limbic system (the vibrational pattern) that resonates with your inherent belief system. If you have been through an in-depth equine assisted training program to integrate coaching, therapy, or simple equine assisted facilitation, you more than likely experienced your own limbic revision in the process. If you are doing your own deep work in the field of equine assisted learning you know, *transformation is not optional!*

As a qualified practitioner of this work, you have already made a leap from one way of being, to an awareness of being different than when you started. You now understand how the seemingly magical encounters with the horse help your clients recognize the existing beliefs and behaviors running their lives. Your ability to guide them to experiment with a new behavior and a new awareness with their horse will compel the horse to shift as well! You are allowing the client to discover their own answers in relationship to another (non-judgmental) being's response to them. You had to go through that same process of transformational awareness to get to a place where you can now hold space for someone else. Kathleen Barry Ingram, (co-founder of the Epona Approach) calls this the "sacred space of possibility."

Now it's time to apply these same principles of transformation to the development of your business. I see many soulful entrepreneurs (with and without horses) separate the way they deliver their service from the way they attempt to build their business. In the delivery of your programs and service you are acutely attuned to your clients and horses, aware and alive in the moment. Then when it comes to matters of building a business, you shift to another part of your brain and cut off all the creative flow and possibilities for what wants to happen next!

It's time to establish new neural pathways with regards to your business and break out the machete of truth to hack away the jungle of overgrown, outdated beliefs preventing your heart's desire! You need a skilled guide with a sharp knife to help you navigate your way out of the jungle and into a new landscape of balance and abundance. There are many resources to choose from, and you do not need to reinvent the wheel! Reading this book and actively participating in the exercises at the end of the chapters is an effective resource I highly recommend!

Do the Work

The best preparation for good work
tomorrow is to do good work today.
—Elbert Hubbard

Do the exercises! There are 7 Lessons created to help you design the business that is the best fit for who you are today. You will be able to access these lessons in the form of a PDF workbook. The first three lessons will focus on who you are (your image/brand), what you do (your expertise) and whom you serve (your ideal client). When these three aspects of your business are in alignment, you will have defined *your own unique signature service*! Then we will take a look at your relationship with money and open some new neural pathways to receive that are in alignment with the value you provide. Finally, the remaining lessons will help you create the program or service that is best suited to support your clients immediately. These 7 lessons are available because reading alone is one the least effective ways to hack your way out of the jungle. The exercises help you embody the concepts into your consciousness, so they become part of how you show up and experience your business in a new way.

Quantum Leap Readiness

Commitment is the ultimate assertion of human
freedom. It releases all the energy you possess and
enables you to take quantum leaps in creativity.
—**Deepak Chopra**

Quantum leap readiness requires an alignment of your three brain centers. Your head (thoughts/intellect), your heart (feelings/intuition) and your gut (actions/impulsion). All three are vital organs of perception that process thoughts and feelings and determine right action. This entire book is structured to help you integrate the alignment of those three brain centers. If your heart says *go* and your head says *no*, your impulsion to act will be half-hearted and incomplete, or no action will take place at all. Like wanting to gallop your horse across the open field, but your head says you're not ready. *He might spook and you could fall off!* Your horse feels your desire to gallop and picks up his pace. You immediately pull on the reins to slow him down. Your messages are incongruent. Your heart feels one thing your head thinks something else. This is confusing to your horse and will likely result in agitation from him. His agitation makes it harder for you to relax and allow the integration of your head and your heart. When you are not in alignment with what you feel and what you think you cannot be an effective leader for your horse or yourself. When you are not in alignment with your head and your heart, you cannot make a quantum leap into the next highest version of your business.

There are 11 important principles and attitudes to embody as you become "quantum leap ready." Your level of embodiment of each attitude determines how soon you will make the next conscious leap into a business that makes a difference for those you serve and serves you and your highest good!

The Principles and Attitudes of Quantum Leap Readiness:
    A Universal Lens (think globally, act locally)
    Curiosity (for possibility)
    High Intention—Low Attachment (to expectations)
    Fierce Love (compassion + forgiveness)
    Trust (the Universe has the net)
    Acceptance (of what is)
    Gratitude (without conditions)
    Humor (amusement for life)
    Discipline (focused desire)
    Courage (aligned action)
    Reciprocal (ability to give and receive)

You can check in with your level of readiness by taking a short assessment available here: schelliwhitehouse.com/qlr/

It will help you to know where you are today as you prepare to become the successful practitioner you have been envisioning as possible!

You may already be well on your way to a new version of your best self. Or you may be taking your first baby steps to prepare yourself. Either way, you are perfect, exactly as you are in this moment. Ready. Willing. Aware.

Shall we leap?

Come to the edge.
We might fall.
Come to the edge.
It's too high!
COME TO THE EDGE!

And they came,
and he pushed,
and they flew.

—**Christopher Logue**

Chapter Three

THE "CART BEFORE THE HORSE"

Your most important work is always
ahead of you, never behind you.
—Stephen Covey

Challenges

While I was outlining the chapters for this book, I carefully planned the order in which the unfolding awareness and action steps would best support your ability to embrace and implement the process. Once I had all the elements in place in the proper order, I wanted to give each step in the process a clever name. Particularly something "horsey" that we could all relate to, like *"7 Strides" to Powerful Program Design* instead of *7 Steps*. Or *"Hit the Trail" to Financial Success* instead of

Follow the Path. And the worst one was, *"Giddyup into Action"* instead of *Align Your* Actions. I'm cringing and laughing at the same time as I share this with you.

The reason why I am sharing this is because it dawned on me that I was trying to force the horse into the process! The design and delivery of our business is our job, not the horse's job. We need to let them do what they do best, and we need to be responsible for making hay.

Get Clients Before You Build a Barn!

> *Having been through the muck and mire,*
> *I've had my own brush with bad choices.*
> —**Michael K. Williams**

We all want the horse to be the star of our work. They are the inspiration for what we do. That's why many of us have invested tens of thousands of dollars into our education, our facilities, and of course our magnificent horses. We are willing do this because we absolutely know the transformational power of experiencing yourself through the eyes of a horse. We are making it our business to bring this work to the public.

However, it's quite possible you have not ever had the pleasure of running your own business. And now you have a vehicle (with horsepower—sorry, couldn't help myself) to truly make a difference in the lives of others and for yourself. If you are a new entrepreneur, or maybe you've been struggling for a while, you may not have the system and structure necessary to reach the people you are meant to serve.

I once had a woman contact me to help her market her new equine assisted coaching business. Andrea (not her real name) left a lucrative, though soul-sucking corporate job to follow her calling to work with horses. She went through a yearlong training program that taught coaching and equine facilitation. She lived on the east coast and had to travel to the west for her week-long training four times that year to the tune of approximately $1500 per trip. Between the cost of the training and travel alone she had invested over $20,000. Andrea didn't own horses when she started the program, but before it was over she had sold her home on the east coast, bought a farm in another state, built a barn, and got three horses!

By the time Andrea reached out to me, she was panicked. She didn't have any clients and had spent most of her savings on what she thought she needed in order to be a successful equine assisted coach. After she related the above story to me her next words were, *I need these horses to start making some money!*

Yikes! This a perfect example of putting the "cart before the horse."

Andrea thought she was building her dream business but she was actually creating a nightmare.

Don't Give Up Your Day Job

Give me six hours to chop down a tree and
I will spend the first four sharpening the axe.
—Abraham Lincoln

If you are just getting started or have been dabbling at this for a while, and you have a job today that pays your bills, don't quit to run off and fulfill your dream of only helping people with your wise and wonderful horses. That's too much stress on you and consequently your horses. Like I said before, you can't just stick a sign out in front of your barn that reads, *Horse Coaching 5¢,* and expect people to start lining up. You need a business designed to support who you are, what you do (with and without horses), and whom you serve in a way that feeds you, your horses, and your bank account!

The good news: it's not rocket science. The bad news: you are the one who is 100% responsible for the success of your practice. Entrepreneurship is not for everyone. I'll say it again: it's the most rigorous personal development journey you will ever encounter. I know how deeply moved and transformed you have become because of your training with the horses.

You Either Will or You Won't

> *He that is good for making excuses*
> *is seldom good for anything else.*
> **—Benjamin Franklin**

I know how enthusiastic you are to assist others in this deep and powerful process of healing and expanding awareness.

So, what's stopping you? I assume you can do the work (or you are learning to do the work) because otherwise, you wouldn't be reading this book.

What is preventing you from inviting people to work with you and getting them to see the value of what you offer?

There are only three possible reasons why you haven't solved this problem for yourself.

1. You don't really want the responsibility for your own business.
2. You don't know the right steps to take and/or in what order you should take them.
3. You don't feel confident that you have what it takes to have a successful equine inspired business.

If the answer is #1, you can stop reading this book now as its sole purpose is to serve anyone who is ready to outline the right steps to build your business and what order you should implement them, and to bust up; dissolve; melt; obliterate the crap that's preventing you from taking the right steps in the right order.

And I want you to know there is nothing wrong with not wanting to own your own business. Entrepreneurship is not for everybody. The early growth to any grand endeavor comes with a lot of uncertainty. Anything you can do to help minimize that uncertainty will go a long way to anchoring long-term success!

I Just Want to Do the Work

There's never a surefire good career move except doing good work.
—Seth Green

When I finished my equine assisted coach training program at the end of 2008 I wanted, more than anything, to go to work for someone who was already facilitating with horses. There were very few practitioners in the state of North Carolina and no equine assisted job board where I could submit my application for hire. God Bless Shannon Knapp and her book, *Horse Sense, Business Sense*. Shannon is a great entrepreneur and set up her equine assisted practice as a serious business right from the beginning. She is incredibly generous with her knowledge and expertise. I recommend Shannon's book for many of the practical aspects necessary to consider for setting up the legal and practical details of your business. She covers topics like liability, insurance, and whether to incorporate. All important stuff.

This book is not that. This book is focused on how to engage with the clients you are meant to serve and quickly generate income. Unless you have a bunch of money socked away for this endeavor, you're going to need to generate income. And not just enough to make ends meet. That's nice for a while, but soon, the "ends" start to pull apart and just aren't meeting anymore. When that happens, anxiety and burnout set in.

I know you just want to do the work and not have to focus on the administrative, organizational, and financial tracking that goes with a growing business. You want to meet the client(s) at the barn, change their lives forever, thank the horses, and go home to a hot meal, a pristine office, and see a note in the morning that lets you know the automatic deposit was made. (Because, who doesn't want that?)

I never wanted to be an entrepreneur. I wanted to show up to someone else's barn and assist them with their awesome program and just do the work (with a paycheck at the end of the week). But there wasn't anybody hiring in my neighborhood, or even in the next state! Most barns didn't have a clue as to what equine assisted coaching was about. If I wanted to do the work, which I did (and do), then I had to figure out a way for people to find me.

I definitely put the "cart before the horse" when I started out. I thought coaching with horses was so cool and so unique that everyone I spoke to would immediately want to schedule a session with me. Ugh, the networking events I slogged through were soul-crushing and not because I didn't meet nice people. It was because I wasn't offering anyone a solution to their problem. I was "forcing the horse" to sell the experience, and, well, that's not their job.

There are more opportunities today to engage in equine facilitated learning than ever before. It is my mission that there will be many, many, many more successful qualified equine assisted providers in the very near future.

I don't want you to give up because it's hard to run a business. Getting through the initial *Holy Crap, I don't know what I'm doing!* phase and knowing the right steps to take in the right order, can turn an unintended nightmare back into a dream come true!

Final Word of Caution

You can be discouraged by failure, or you can learn from it.
So go ahead and make mistakes, make all you can.
Because, remember that's where you'll find success—
on the far side of failure.
—Thomas J. Watson

Anything worth doing takes effort, focus, and dedication. You already put the time and investment and dedication into your education. The crafting of a business that is a true reflection of you and the horse work deserves the same amount of time, investment, and dedication— probably more. This isn't a job. It's your life and your lifestyle. When I'm out with the horses and my clients, I almost have to pinch myself I'm so overcome with gratitude. I love it when people arrive to the barn for the first time and I say, "Welcome to my office! Come meet the team," and then I introduce them to the horses. I am so freakin' privileged to have a life like this!

Because of the pioneers in this industry that have gone before you, I hope you won't have to work as hard or wait as long for sustainable success. The tools and strategy exist now. You are the only obstacle to your horse and soul success!

And don't tell me you can't afford marketing or mentoring or whatever it is you believe you can't afford. If it is important enough to you, you will make it happen. And sometimes, that's the kind of skin you need to commit to the game if you want to truly break through the fear of whatever is holding you back.

And guess what else, you don't need a website or a big mailing list or even a business card to get started. If you're focused on the "exterior" of your business first, then it's going to be a lot more expensive in the long run to get up and going. I know, because I did it that way and got sucked into a big expensive website rabbit hole that all went to hell anyway. This is what I mean by 'get clients first, then build the barn'!

The Hardest Job You'll Ever Love

> *A dream doesn't become reality through magic;*
> *it takes sweat, determination and hard work.*
> **—Colin Powell**

Entrepreneurship is a big inside job. It's all about you. You don't have a boss to blame for crappy tools or infrastructure or client engagement. Much of your business will be run by a committee, the "Me, Myself and I" committee that has 1001 reasons why it's not possible to have the kind of business you want. Oh, the committee is all in on the vision of what you want, they just don't know how to make it happen. So, they'll come up with excuses for why you can't do whatever it is you need to do.

Remember when Trump became president and after about two weeks he said in a speech, "This job is hard!"? You are now the president of your business. Every decision, every success, every, every, everything is your responsibility. You can approach this new chapter in your life with curiosity for what's possible and embrace the freedom to make your own choices and create your own success, or not.

It's a lot more fun if you do!

Chapter Four

YOUR IMAGE

---

*I think that dwelling on other people's
perception of you is the road to complete madness.*
—Kate Beckinsale

How the World Sees You

When you are an entrepreneur, you are putting yourself up on your own pedestal. Oh, I know that might have made your hackles go up, but hang in there. It's not a pedestal of public or self-adoration. You are stepping out into an arena of other transformational service providers and saying to the world, *I have something special that will change your life!* If you do not somehow rise up, show up, and stand out, how is anyone to know you are there to help them?

It takes a lot of courage to step away from the crowd and share a unique voice that may be "untested" in your circle of expertise. What if you say the wrong thing and get embarrassed? Or worse, you embarrass someone you care about by stepping out of the status quo.

How many people do you honestly know that do not care one iota what anyone else thinks of them? I throw down a challenge to anyone that says they do not care what others think of them. Except for the Dalai Lama. I believe him. I saw an extraordinary interview on March 5th, 2017, with the Dalai Lama conducted by John Oliver of the HBO comedy news show, *Last Week Tonight*.

The Dalai Lama's View

In the practice of tolerance, one's enemy is the best teacher.
—Dalai Lama

China has openly slandered the Dalai Lama and even gone so far as banning any US citizen from entering China if they have previously met with the Dalai Lama. Lady Gaga's concert was cancelled because she met with the Dalai Lama publicly to discuss yoga!

The country of Tibet is nearly a quarter of the size of China and has been brutally attacked by China since the 1950's. Hundreds of thousands of people have been killed along with the destruction of hundreds of Buddhist monasteries. The Dalai Lama is the prime spiritual leader of Tibet and has been in exile since 1959, tirelessly working to share his message of peace all while his country and his people are experiencing horrific atrocities. This man has an entire government that hates him. John Oliver read a statement by a Chinese official that called the Dalai Lama "A wolf in monk's robes." The Dalai Lama laughed and said, "Yes, they see me as a demon." He said he feels no negative feelings about what they call him. He just has feelings of love about that. He went on to say, "I practice taking others anger, suspicion, distrust and give them patience, tolerance and compassion."

Here is a man who is seen and portrayed as a demon to billions of people in China, and yet, to billions and billions more people he is a walking representation of patience, tolerance, and compassion.

I offer this extreme example to illustrate that, no matter who you really are, and how magnificent your intentions are—others can only see you according to their own perceptions based on their own conditioned way of thinking.

A 360 Degree View

There is no truth. There is only perception.
—Gustave Flaubert

Maybe you've experienced a 360 Profile assessment or something similar. Your colleagues (or friends and family) fill out an anonymous survey based on their experience of interacting with you. Many businesses use these profile assessments to determine interpersonal strengths and weaknesses in their management teams. How other people experience you is useful information in this context. You may find out some helpful things about what is working in your professional relationships and where you might improve. As thorough as these assessments try to be, they cannot possibly be accurate to the extent that they portray a reflection of who you really are. The feedback is from others who experience you in a role you fulfill, based on someone else's expectations and their perception of how that role should be fulfilled.

As business owners, we tend to spend a lot of energy on wondering what people think about us and our service. We can receive 100 glowing testimonials, and 1 snotty, unhappy client makes a rude comment, and we go into a tailspin for days. We care about how others perceive us even though their perception is not actually about us. It's about them.

How the world sees you is not what's important in connecting the soul of your business to the heart of clients. How you see yourself is what makes all the difference!

The False Self

> *It's not who you are that holds you back,*
> *it's who you think you're not.*
> **—Author Unknown**

During my coach training we went through an in-depth discussion about the False Self versus the Authentic Self. We were given a blank paper plate and a marker and asked to draw the face that we show the world. I drew a smile and a wink to illustrate, *I got this!* The happy, confident face that let's others know there's nothing to worry about everything is handled.

On the back of the plate we wrote down all the things we actually say to ourselves inside our head.

Crap, I don't know what I'm doing.
I'm not smart enough to be a coach.
Who do I think I am?
Why would anyone hire me?
I don't belong here.
I've never succeeded at anything.
I'm such a loser.

I would've written more, but the instructor called time. The exercise left me shaky and nauseous. Then oh joy, we got to go around the circle with our masks in front of our face and read our statements out loud. The words barely got out in between the sobs. I felt raw and exposed. As I listened to what the others had written, I was shocked that they could possibly believe some of the horrible things they said about themselves. My experience of them was completely opposite of those statements. Particularly my mentors, Lisa Murrell and Linda Kohanov, who I saw as perfect and amazing! Linda had written two wildly successful books, *The Tao of Equus* and *Riding Between the Worlds*, and was working on her third book! I was at her remarkable ranch outside of Tucson, AZ, with her magnificent herd of horses. My perception was, *She is perfect; she must be so happy.* And then there was Lisa. A beautiful, smart woman who just launched the first International Coach Federation accredited coach training program in the world that included horses! How could either of them have any of the same self-flagellating thoughts about themselves that I held for myself? Hadn't they overcome self-doubt? They had already proven their talent and value to the world!

Two realizations whammed me at once. One, I was relieved to find out that everyone has "false self" thoughts. Second was, *Oh, shit. You mean I'm going to have these thoughts about myself forever?*

The Authentic Self

> *There is but one cause of human failure.*
> *And that is man's lack of faith in his true Self.*
> **—William James**

Fast-forward about five years to 2014, I became a facilitator and adjunct teacher in the Equine Alchemy Coach Certification Training program. The "False Self" exercise was still an integral aspect of the training: especially, when working with horses. As a coach, it is imperative that we show up as congruent as possible. Meaning, what we think, how we feel, and what we are doing are in clear alignment. It's the only way we can hold the sacred container required for clients to see themselves as clearly as the horse will see them.

One day, while co-facilitating the False exercise (for about the 30th time) I realized that, while jotting down the negative self-talk, I felt really angry. There was another voice inside my head and she was saying,

This is boring.

You are not that.

Stop saying those things!

It was the first time the self-flagellation failed to trigger tears. It was another experience of witnessing myself move out of the lower vibration of "not good enough" to a higher vibration of "good enough." There was a bit of a yo-yo effect for a while as I had to get used to not having awful thoughts about myself as the predominant messages in my head! *If I am not the loser I have believed myself to be, who am I?*

Who am I, really?

What do I stand for?

How do I make a difference?

I had asked myself these questions many times. But the answers had always been governed by the *I'm not good enough* filter. The *I'm an imposter* message kept me from experiencing myself the way that others experienced me. I showed up. I did good work. I was enthusiastic, caring, creative, innovative, motivated, and loved my work and the people I helped. I received a lot of loving feedback and yet, I did not experience myself as others experienced me.

If you are caught in a similar cycle of negative self-talk you are most likely undercharging for your services, deflecting praise (and likely compensation as well), and putting your dreams aside because of the belief that you could never be the one to have the success you see others enjoy.

The Cranky Ego

Self-criticism is not "love," and it is certainly not indifferent. It's a form of hatred. And when I name that, when I see it for what it is (raw and uncomfortable and saddening), when I refuse to sugar-coat self- criticism, judgment, agitation, and constantly trying to improve myself, then I'm one quantum leap closer to freedom.
—**Danielle LaPorte**

In case you're wondering, the False Self never goes away. You will know the False Self as its message is always, always, always, negative. Some call it the Ego, but I believe the Ego has a different role. I believe the Ego is that aspect of our identity that has a fixed perception of who we are and how we need to show up in the world to stay emotionally safe. Our Ego is the representational behavior of past programming and wants to align itself with the operating system it already knows. Even if that operating system is outdated and no longer serves you, it still serves the Ego.

When you step into the next highest version of who you really are, you need to show up differently to "be" the person who lives at that higher vibration. The Ego is likely to pick a fight with you every time over that new way of being! The Ego will very often align itself with the False Self and jump on the "who-do-you-think-you-are bandwagon" in its desperate attempt to have you get back in line to where it is comfortable again.

In preparation for a quantum leap into the next highest version of your business, I want you to have a strong grasp of the difference between the False Self and the Ego to be able to navigate the flood of "fake news" they will use to manipulate your emotions. You must learn to communicate with them in a clear and powerful way if you want others to know and experience you in the way you wish to show up and be seen.

I Am That

My life is basically my work.
—Temple Grandin

At the beginning of this chapter we talked about how the Dalai Lama was able take the hate projected onto him and give back patience, tolerance, and compassion. I'm going to make a bold statement here, since I haven't asked the Dalai Lama directly. I bet he experiences himself as a patient, tolerant, and compassionate human being. It is his practice to be mindful of those states of consciousness. He cannot control how others will project their agendas or insecurities upon him. He can control how he receives their energy and gives his energy back.

As a teacher of patience, tolerance, and compassion he diligently practices those qualities and characteristics until they become him.

The qualities and characteristics of quantum leap readiness are to prepare you to embody the person you say you want to be. Once you can clearly identify your False Self and your Ego, you will be open to hear your Authentic Self, the voice of your Soul calling you forward to build the life that is in alignment with your true essence!

Your Present Results Are the Mirror of Your Past Perceptions

The problem is that perception is reality.
—John Rowland

It will be infinitely harder to implement the practical details of building and sustaining a successful equine assisted business if you don't know who you really are, what you stand for, and what solution you provide for others.

Here is a reminder of the Quantum Leap Principles and Attitudes we will be integrating throughout the book:

A Universal Lens (think globally, act locally)
Curiosity (for possibility)
High Intention—Low Attachment (to expectations)
Fierce Love (compassion + forgiveness)
Trust (the Universe has the net)
Acceptance (of what is)
Gratitude (without conditions)
Humor (amusement for life)
Discipline (focused desire)
Courage (aligned action)
Reciprocal (ability to give and receive)

If you have come through a rigorous training to be able to facilitate the nuanced work with the magnificent horse, then I am going to assume that on some level you are already working to actively integrate these principles and qualities into your work with clients and hopefully in building your business structure as well.

The results you are presently experiencing in your business are the most accurate barometer of where you are with regards to how you experience your true self. You are either showing up in your authentic power, and giving and receiving in alignment with your gifts and talents, or you are not. Or maybe you're experiencing the yo-yo effect of "almost there" and you just need a little hand-holding to get you past the internal naysayers.

Let's go ahead, and go to the next level, shall we?

Remember, this is your life to create. It's yours to make up as you go.

It's all an illusion anyway so you might as well make it a good one!
—Jack Canfield

 Lesson: The Core of Your Purpose
Access Link: https://schelliwhitehouse.com/bch/

Why You Should Do This Exercise...
The Core of Your Purpose lesson is an opportunity for you uncover your true essence: who you really are, no matter what! The first foundational ingredient to aligning the soul of your equine assisted business to the heart of your clients.

---––– *Chapter Five* –––---

WHAT YOU DO

As far as we can discern, the sole purpose of human existence
is to kindle a light in the darkness of mere being.
—Carl Jung

Your Expertise

You are a soulful entrepreneur. You are your business and your business is you. The magic you create with horses is an extension of who you are. The good, the bad, and the beautiful!

It's important for you to be in alignment with who you are and what you offer in a way that feels valid and amazing. You don't need to be a braggart. You do need to articulate the value of your service from your authentic self and know the power of what you have to offer in a way that resonates through everything you do.

Your service, your expertise, your stand in the world all come from your core. The essence of what you came into the world to be.

Who Are You—No Matter What?

Why are you trying so hard to fit in,
when you're born to stand out?
—Oliver James

In the exercise from the last chapter you identified your *raison d'etre*, your reason for being. Now I'm going to ask you, "Who are you, no matter what?"

Who are you? Outside of anything and everything you've ever done or accomplished in the world—who are you?

The first time I was asked that question I was totally taken aback. What do you mean, "Who am I?" I'm a mom, a wife, a daughter, a sister, a granddaughter, a coach, a horsewoman, and so on.... And perhaps you are those things too. But that is not who you are at your essence.

Outside of the roles you fulfill and the degrees you've earned and the failures you've endured and the mountains you've climbed, who are you?

What is your essence? How do your friends or other loved ones describe you? Are you romantic, silly, soulful, serious, outrageous, brave, fun, carefree, dark, earthy, colorful, eccentric, heady, brilliant, ditzy, wise, cautious, creative, tasteful, outlandish, thoughtful, and I think you get the point. Your essence is not only how you experience yourself, it is reflected in how other people experience you.

Be You, Through and Through

Authenticity is everything! You have to wake up every day and look in the mirror, and you want to be proud of the person who's looking back

at you. And you can only do that if you're being honest with yourself
and being a person of high character.

You have an opportunity every single day
to write that story of your life.
—**Aaron Rodgers**

If you are trying to create a business that markets to executive
CEO's of engineering companies and your essence shines through
as a carefree, spontaneous creative, one of two things is going to
transpire, and you're not going to like either of them. One: you will
clearly not be the right match for their company and not get the
job. Two: you bluff your way into the gig and then find you are
miserable because they don't get you and you don't get them. They
are not getting the results they were looking for, and your super
powers are swirling down the drain, totally unrecognized. Honor
your essence. Celebrate your uniqueness and build your business
from that place. Isn't that why you want to have your own business,
so you can experience the freedom to express yourself through your
work? Trying to behave like someone that you really aren't creates a
misalignment within the head/heart/gut continuum, and you know,
when you are not in alignment with yourself, no one else can align
with you either!

During my certification course for marketing we went through a
simple exercise to help get in touch with our personal essence. The core
of who we are no matter what. I was elated! I felt as if I'd found the Holy
Grail. I am the essence of fun and freedom, and it felt oh, so right to
acknowledge that. I tried to tweak it and make it more mysterious and
deep, but the truth is "fun and freedom" ring true for me.

The essence of who I am, no matter what, is the feeling I strive to
maintain in my work and life. Everything I say yes to has to go through

the fun and freedom filter. If it's not fun, I don't want to do it. If it restricts my freedom of self-expression, well, that's not fun.

If I want to live a life that expresses my unique essence, then my work needs to be structured around fun and freedom! That's when I realized there was no turning back. I was going to have to launch my own business. There just weren't any job openings offering fun and freedom packages with benefits and 401K's.

Who You Were Born to Be

When you tune into your Soul essence and are in harmony with
the Supreme, you are tapped into your superpowers.
—**Sharon Kirstin**, *The Answers Within*

What are you really, really good at? What comes so naturally that you hardly have to think about it? It could be anything. Let's start with what you were born with. What did people say about you when you were younger that you can identify with? "Oh, she is so good with animals." "He is an excellent student." "She was always the creative one." This would be a good time to pick up your journal and jot down some of those things.

Next, make a list of the things that you've become good at through your own determination and effort. Where have you focused 10,000 hours of your blood, sweat, tears, and brain cells to become the best you can be at this point in your life? Again, this can be anything in addition to your equine assisted training. You might be an expert at parenthood, music, or foreign languages. Perhaps you've become a master coach, healer, therapist, doctor, photographer, artist, writer, journalist, teacher, inventor, scientist, entrepreneur, marketer, weaver, programmer, builder, lawyer, fighter pilot, or mechanic. Maybe you are a world class athlete (or striving to become one), a dancer, equestrian, juggler, or comedian. You may already be a CEO of a major company. You might be amazing at many things. It's important to identify and acknowledge your dedication to mastering something important to you, whether you were born with an aptitude for it or not.

Your expertise does not stand alone. It is flavored and supported by your essence and by the many other things you are either already good at, or you are striving to master and integrate into your highest and best self. How you grow and learn about yourself and what you provide for others is part of your expertise. It's an aspect of how you hold others capable and accountable to their own personal development.

The integration of your essence and your expertise gives you a super genius that no one else can claim. Give that super genius a platform to stand upon, and the people you are meant to serve will finally be able to find you!

Your Stand

> *It takes a great deal of bravery to stand up to our enemies,*
> *but just as much to stand up to our friends.*
> **—J. K. Rowling**

What do you stand for no matter what?

There are two components to this question. Both components require that you take a stand. The first component is, *what do you stand for in your life?* This includes your community, your family and your own well-being. The second component is, *what are you no longer willing to tolerate in your life?*

Your stand is how you show up every day. What do people count on you for? What are you the go-to person for? Do others count on you to have the most rational solutions? Are you the peace maker or negotiator? Do others look to you for clarity or organization?

Your stand is often the qualities that others most seek from you. They know you stand in that authentic place of knowing what to do about a particular situation. My personal stand is for the unique expression of the Soul. I believe this why people pour their hearts out to me. They know (without me saying anything) that I am a safe place for them to be seen and heard. That's who I am. I just came that way. My business is a natural extension of my stand.

Tolerate No More

> *All the world is full of suffering. It is also full of overcoming.*
> —**Helen Keller**

The second component to knowing what you are a stand for, is knowing what you can no longer tolerate. Notice I did not say, knowing what you stand for is knowing what you stand against. Resistance to anything gives power and strength to the very thing you are resisting. Perhaps you struggle with social injustices, pollution, discrimination, or animal abuse. Your power is standing in what you are for and creating the space for solutions to what you can no longer tolerate.

Note in your journal what you know you stand for and what you can no longer tolerate in your personal life, your community, and the world. To clearly identify what you can no longer tolerate offers a clue as to who you are meant to support and serve through your work with the horses.

Who Are You Being Today?

> *The thing is most people are afraid to step out,*
> *to take a chance beyond their established identity.*
> —**Demi Moore**

So far in your journal, you should have a few notes on the expertise, talents, and skills that you have mastered or are consciously developing. You should also have some notes on what you are a stand for and what you are no longer willing to tolerate. Take a few moments to consider how you are expressing those skills and talents today? When you became an equine assisted practitioner did you throw out everything you learned in your corporate job because you hated that environment and now you just want to have enlightened people come and stand in the field with you and your horses and experience love and healing?

Or in the case of a therapist or mental health professional, you might be trying to force a new, expanded model of doing business into an old formula that doesn't allow you to charge what you are worth even though you now have the added expense of your equine partners to consider.

I worked with a bright and enthusiastic woman named Pia Liesmann who was just launching her equine assisted coaching career.

She was already an executive coach and wanted to incorporate horses into her offerings. When she was nearing the end of her training we started working on her business development and came to realize that she had a real expertise for dealing with Attention Deficit Disorder. Her husband and one of her sons both experienced ADD. She had a lot of empathy for people who care for and deal with loved ones who are suffering with ADD/ADHD. Her coaching skills gave her some excellent tools, and what she learned through the horses opened up a whole new vein to help others learn to manage moods and accountability much more quickly than the talk therapy they had been experiencing.

Pia examined her natural abilities and her expertise through training and/or experience. She identified her stand for clear and conscious communication and recognized that she was no longer going to tolerate parents and caretakers not having access to a harmonious relationship with their children or spouses! I'll share Pia's success with her revelation in the next chapter.

Offer Relief

Can I see another's woe, and not be in sorrow too?
Can I see another's grief, and not seek for kind relief?
—William Blake

By now I hope you are beginning to understand that our magnificent horses, that make our work feel magical, are not the foundation of our business. They are a super awesome feature and an incredible addition to helping your clients know and understand themselves. But almost no one is typing "coaching with horses" into their search engines in search of solving their problem.

Your future clients are typing "how to cope with my ADHD kid," "how to get a fair divorce," "how to lose weight," "how do I stop being sad," "what to do about my hair loss," "I don't know how to talk to my teenagers," "how to start a business," "how do I find a boyfriend," "how to experience God," "why do I get so angry," and so on. People are looking for solutions to their problem. They want to know how to get from the uncomfortable situation they are experiencing right now, to not being uncomfortable anymore.

Show them that you are the person with a solution to their problem, and they will happily step into the arena with you, even if they are terrified of horses. Because they are more terrified of what their life will become if they don't solve their problem!

You possess the ability to help solve someone's problem. Make a commitment to find out what that is and you will have gratifying work for you and your herd for years to come!

Our job in this life is not to shape ourselves into
some ideal we imagine we ought to be, but to
find out who we already are and become it.
—**Stephen Pressfield**, *The War of Art*

 Lesson: Claim Your Super Power
Access Link: https://schelliwhitehouse.com/bch/

Why You Should Do This Exercise…

The purpose of this exercise is to help you connect the intersections between who you really are and both your natural and learned abilities. There's a sweet spot of expertise there that is your unique superpower!

Chapter Six

YOUR PROMISE

*Keep every promise you make and
only make promises you can keep.*
—Anthony Hitt

The experience you offer through your work with horses is an extension of who you are, your expertise, and the promise you make to take a stand for your clients. That promise is to help them solve a problem.

Pia's Promise

*No one is rewarded more richly in time, space, or beyond,
than the person who has helped others. And it matters*

not whether they helped selflessly or selfishly, for a profit
or for free, with an Apple or a Droid. Help is help,
—*The Universe* (**Mike Dooley**)

Remember, my client Pia who realized she had a lot of experience with ADD/ADHD people and wanted to help other people enjoy a more harmonious relationship with their ADD/ADHD loved ones? She didn't have a PhD in psychology or behavioral science. She is a great coach and equine facilitator who happens to have a lot of experience and empathy for people and families dealing with ADD/ADHD.

Based on her experience, she quickly put together a simple five-chapter e-book about living with ADD/ADHD family members and shared it with a local women's group. That resulted in an invitation to speak to a whole gathering of parents who have ADD/ADHD children! That was fantastic. Now we needed to create her offer. Because of course, after she presents her experience and introduces the coping skills she learned through working with horses, people in the audience were going to want to know how to work with her!

Pia had shared with me that she really wanted to work with the parents and caregivers of ADD/ADHD children. She had wished she had someone to help her when her son was younger, and she was discovering her husband had adult ADD/ADHD!

She was thinking that once the parents had a session with the horses that she would offer to continue coaching to support the learning and process of managing emotions and responses.

This type of offer is a common (unconscious) mistake that practitioners often make. It's understandable that you would like a client to have a powerful experience with you that helps them to see they can have more powerful experiences if they continue to work with you. It can work out that way, some of the time.

There are two scenarios to this dilemma:

- You may have an amazing session with the horses and your client. You let them know you are going to follow-up with them in a couple of days to see how they are doing and talk about how you can go forward together. But after they go away, they sometimes wonder if the seemingly miraculous experience they had with the horse was just a fluke or a coincidence. They will start to doubt or even feel a bit foolish that they put so much trust in a "dumb animal." When you call to follow up with them and invite them to continue coaching, instead of a resounding "Yes," you are likely going to spend time undoing the doubts and default way of thinking that crept back over them. This may or may not result in another coaching session, but it's a lot work and not very productive for the client.
- The second scenario is to offer continued coaching at the end of the first session when they are open and receptive. This puts a lot of pressure on you as a practitioner to create a space to 'sell' more coaching. The work with the horses can often be deep and emotionally unsettling for some people. They may be feeling vulnerable as they are learning to trust new information about themselves. At this point, trying to introduce your coaching package options takes them out of their newly opened heart space and back into their heads.

Caveat: There are appropriate times to discuss ongoing coaching during demo sessions, workshops and within existing coaching contracts. But not during or at the end of an actual client session.

Please don't beat yourself up if have been doing this or thought it was a good way to let someone get a 'taste' of your work before inviting them to continue. At first glance, it appears perfectly logical.

What Do Your Clients Want More
Than Anything in the World?

Help others achieve their dreams and you will achieve yours.
—Les Brown

I asked Pia what she thought those parents and caregivers want more than anything in the world. She replied, "They want their children to know how to thrive in world that doesn't understand them." Then I asked, "Where are they most likely to invest their money, in helping their child or helping themselves?" Of course, you know the answer is helping their child. Pia was a little dismayed by this realization because she was passionate about helping the parents.

Knowing that the parents were going to ask her about bringing their children to work with the horses was a fantastic first step. The second step was to create an offer that would not only provide the service they were seeking, but provide an even greater service that would benefit them far more significantly than they could have imagined!

When parents approach her after her talk to ask if she could work with their children she could say, "Yes, of course! I have a very specific program that supports both you and your child."

Pia made it a policy that she did not work with any children without their parents working with her as well. Her introductory program included three sessions with the horses, one with the parents, one with the child and one with the family together. In between each session was a coaching call with the parents to help them deepen and forward the learning. The horse sessions and phone sessions had to be completed within an 8- week time frame to develop constructive momentum and not allow the ADD/ADHD dramas to 'string things out".

Now Pia had a viable program that would support the people she most wanted to help (the parents) as well as give them the opportunity support the social development of their child (what they want more than anything else in the world)!

What Do You Do for You?

Work is our Love made visible.
—Kahlil Gibran

When we first explored working with ADD/ADHD families, Pia was conflicted. Her focus and resume were built on executive and team coaching. The whole time she was going through equine assisted coach training she was constructing a plan to bring executives and their teams into the woo-woo arena of horse wisdom. She knew there was money for experiential learning there, and that was certainly a population that could benefit from building up some empathy skills!

She had the coaching chops to facilitate an executive team but at the time she was going to need to do some legwork to find a facility with enough horses to support that kind of experience and another qualified equine assisted practitioner and horse handlers to help her deliver the experience.

We looked at all the facts first:

- She was new to coaching with horses and had not yet facilitated teams.
- She only had one horse she could work with when she first began.
- She had limited hours to do the work because of extreme climate conditions (she lives in Dubai).

- She wanted to establish her work with horses quickly to keep honing her skills.

Once all the pieces of the puzzle were in front of us, a new picture emerged which allowed Pia to launch her equine assisted coaching practice with more ease and joy than she had imagined!

Remember: Do the Work!

You feel alive to the degree that you feel you can help others.
—**John Travolta**

When I was going through my coach training program in 2008, we did an exercise where we drew a picture of the future of our business on a big flip chart. I was so excited to share my grand vision of a beautiful farm with all the state of the art equine facilities, happy horses, cabins for clients, and other thought leaders who would come to experience the work and share it with others. A big lake and a giant fire pit and a partner to help me bring it all to fruition. Imagine all of that drawn out with stick figures and no sense of proportion. That was my drawing.

I had basically described Linda Kohanov's facility, which at the time was Apache Springs Ranch. A magnificent 100 acre spread in Sonoita, AZ, with everything I described above and more. Numerous employees and volunteers to manage. Multiple events taking place every week. And marketing and client care required to keep the place going. It was a huge operation.

After I finished my happy little presentation, Linda leaned over, stared me in the eye, and said, "Schelli, just do the work."

What? No applause. No pat on the back for an amazing vision. "Just do the work."

At the time, I didn't really know what that meant. I went home and continued to focus on my dream of my own facility. I named it "The Center of Possibility". I got Jim Horan's book, *The One Page Business Plan*, found someone to help me identify my strengths, weaknesses, opportunities and threats, and discovered all I needed was $1.5 million to launch the business of my dreams. (ROFL!)

I didn't know back then that I could've spent less than 2 months with a program design coach to help me get started right away and "just do the work." Instead I spent hours and hours creating a business plan that didn't have any real clients in it. And no advice on how to find real clients. I was busy, busy, busy designing "The Center of Possibilities" from the "build it and they will come" mentality.

I still have that dream, and over the years much of it has manifested in the most unexpected ways! However, it has manifested as a result of me doing the work and becoming the person who creates "The Center of Possibilities" for all of the people who are showing up, not the other way around.

Pia's focus on what she could do right away gave her business momentum and gave her the opportunity to do the work! Instead of spending months working on landing an executive contract, lining up additional facilities and practitioners, she simply offered her expertise to people she cared about who were right in front of her. She got to work.

She showed up as an equine assisted coach, people learned about her work and she was eventually contacted by another executive coach asking Pia to bring the horse work to their clients! And that coaching firm arranged all the extra details!

Pia Creates World Peace

*Some people still make promises and keep those they make. When
they do, they help make life around them more stably human.*
—**Lewis B. Smedes**

Every action we take, or don't take has an impact on ourselves, our
family, our community, and the world. As I said before, my mission is
to raise consciousness in the world. If you ask me why I want to raise
consciousness, I will tell you, "It's because I want the animals to be
happy, even the human animals."

Raising our collective level of consciousness does not erase default
assumptions of self-doubt, prejudice, or ingrained social beliefs and fears.
It brings awareness to their existence so that we can make a different
choice about how to respond in every moment. Horses are the super
guru Zen masters of how to live in the present moment. But you already
know that. It's the millions and millions of people waking up around
the planet that need your support to bring them to this phenomenal
experience of getting to truly know themselves and not have the rest of
their lives fall apart all around them.

Pia wasn't consciously aware of each of the quantum leap principles
as she was diligently working through the process of how she wanted to
incorporate who she really is, with her career and her lifestyle. And there
was plenty of "what if" worries and battles with her false self. But in the
end, the results came from her commitment to follow her heart and trust
that her instincts will provide for her highest good. Her embodiment
of the quantum leap principles prepared her for the quantum leap
opportunity that was presented to her as a result of showing up and
doing the work. This is a snapshot of how the principles supported her
quantum leap readiness:

A Universal Lens (think globally, act locally)—she too wants to raise consciousness in the world through coaching and horses. She started with one family, one horse, one offer.

Curiosity (for possibility)—she got curious about other potential opportunities that weren't related to her original goal.

High Intention—Low Attachment (to expectations)—she had a high intention of landing a big corporate fish. She realized she needed to let go of her attachment to the timeline for catching one of those big fish.

Fierce Love (compassion + forgiveness)—Pia had a strong compassionate love for the ADD/ADHD community and sincerely wanted to make a difference.

Trust (the Universe has the net)—she trusted her own coaching and facilitation abilities, and she trusted that if it was meant to be, the right people would show up.

Acceptance (of what is)—she accepted where she was in her business and took action from that place.

Gratitude (without conditions)—she was grateful for all she was experiencing in the process, even the hard bits.

Humor (amusement for life)—she was able to laugh at her own doubts and misgivings about not being a qualified 'mental health' practitioner.

Discipline (focused desire)—she created a plan to offer assistance to people who needed it and then followed through by scheduling time for each action that needed to be implemented.

Courage (aligned action)—it took courage to show up in a room full of strangers and tell her story and offer assistance despite the doubts and fears!

Reciprocal (ability to give and receive)—she created a high value container that provided real momentum for her clients in exchange for a price that reflected that value of the solution! Everybody was happy.

Who Are You Meant to Serve?

> *For a long time, I was looking for my perfect*
> *equilibrium, my mojo. And now I think I'm getting*
> *there: I've found my customer, my silhouette, my cut.*
> **—Alexander McQueen**

We know that 20 minutes in the round pen can get to the heart of an issue blocking someone's momentum faster than weeks or even months of talking can reveal. We don't want to leave anyone out of the opportunity to work with us. However, if you're talking to everyone, no one is listening.

More than anything in this crazy, busy, flashy world, people want to be seen and heard and understood. Pia spoke to a very specific group of people, parents with ADD/ADHD children. She had the talent and the skill set to coach corporate executives as well, and that opportunity eventually came to her even though she was focused on serving a different need.

Personally, the small collective of people I most want to serve is you. You are the soulful entrepreneur I most want to lift up and get your message out to those who are ready to engage with you. I know our efforts with the horses are contributing to the healing of the consciousness of this planet.

The principles, teachings, and philosophies in this book could be applied to any soulful service practice, but my mission is to help you reach more people as quickly as possible in a way that is meaningful to you and makes a difference to those you serve.

The next exercise, *Claim Your Clients*, will help you connect with who you are ready to serve now. If you're just beginning it may be a very narrow group of people to invite into your program. Even if you already have a specific demographic of people you serve, this exercise may help you see where you can expand your offerings or branch into another area of expertise.

> *Devote yourself to holding space for people to*
> *be themselves, which means being different.*
> **—Eric Coppolino**

 Lesson: Claim Your Clients Exercise
Access Link: https://schelliwhitehouse.com/bch/

Why You Should Do This Exercise...
Claiming and connecting to your ideal client is the single most important focus of a successful business. If you're talking to everyone, no one is listening. This exercise helps you determine your ideal client based on your core values, your expertise, and the problem that needs to be solved for those you are meant to serve.

Chapter Seven

YOUR BELIEFS

The sun was shining on the sea,
Shining with all his might:
He did his very best to make
The billows smooth and bright –
And this was odd, because it was
The middle of the night.
—Lewis Carroll

Our actions are all for naught when operating in the dark: Are you really in business if no one comes and pays you for your service? If you *believe* you are doing everything possible to grow your practice and yet you are not generating the income you need and desire, then you are *believing the wrong thing*!

If Wishes Were Horses

> *Hope is being able to see that there*
> *is light despite all of the darkness.*
> **—Desmond Tutu**

There is a phrase I remembered while writing this, *"If wishes were horses beggars would ride."* When I was a kid I played that phrase over and over in my head, trying to reason what it meant.

Now I know it is meant to imply that wishes are hard to fulfill. Everyone has many wishes (and hopes and desires), and if every wish manifested as a horse (for some of us they do!), everyone would ride, including those who seemingly have little resources.

My question to you is, "If wishes were horses ... would you ride?"

As I was looking at our cultural beliefs around money that phrase kept popping into my head. What IF wishes were horses—would the beggars actually ride them? Would you?

Think about this for a minute....

We all wish for more, bigger, better, faster, slimmer, sleeker, smarter, richer... something-er in our lives. But here's the rub... sometimes it's right in front you (or maybe right behind you), and you don't even notice it. Or you give it a passing glance and think 'it's not for you' because ... because ... because!

Why isn't it for you?

My theory is most of the beggars who would be surrounded by beautiful wish-fulfilled horses would never ride one. They would not believe that horse was for them, that it could be true! They cannot imagine themselves as the person who lives the experience they wish for. Their belief is they cannot have what they see others enjoying. Because our experience is always a projection of our deepest, mostly unconscious beliefs, the majority of the beggars would not ride.

Vibrational Matches Not Made in Heaven

When what you value and dream about doesn't
match the life you are living, you have pain."
—**Shannon L. Alder**

Mike Dooley of *Notes from the Universe* is famous for saying, "Thoughts Become Things." He's talking about the fact that our thoughts are literally energy. Energy is vibration. Therefore, our thoughts create a vibration. That vibration is the equivalent of a request to the Universe for the vibrational image to manifest into a tangible experience. Whether that experience is material or experiential makes no difference. Whether the thought is positive or negative makes no difference.

All of that is fantastic and was the foundation of the book and the movie, *The Secret.* That one concept inspired millions of people (including me) to create vision boards and positive affirmations in an earnest attempt to vibrate with the car, boyfriend, house, job, bank account (you name it) of their dreams!

The Law of Vibration (Attraction) is one of several Universal Truths, and in theory the above practice of aligning your thoughts with what you want, instead of what you don't want, should bring your heart's desire into existence!

There's one small problem, we humans have more than one operating system manning our energetic vibration. There is a default operating system that was programmed from the time we were born until approximately age six or seven years old. This is the age when we begin to discern fact from fiction and notice the hypocrisies all around us. Note that I said begin to notice fact from fiction. Some pull away from their cultural programming later than others. Some never do. Regardless, the programming is still installed and can never be uninstalled. It can however be recognized as an integral part of your overall operating system and become a choice as opposed to a default.

Who Gave You That Idea?

> *It's not the events of our lives that shape us,*
> *but our beliefs as to what those events mean.*
> —**Tony Robbins**

Psychological research tells us that, before the age of six years old, we are primarily little human sponges absorbing everything in our environment as fact. We do not have the cognitive ability to reason or filter out untruths. It's why we so readily believe in Santa Claus and the Easter Bunny. Our parents and guardians have told us these beings exist and provide evidence for us to "experience" them as real.

I totally struggled with whether or not to propagate the Santa Claus myth when my first child was born. I did not want to tell her a lie. My husband was adamant that she not be the only kid who doesn't believe in Santa Claus and ruin it for all the other kids. So, I caved and agreed that we would lie to our daughter, and then our son too of course. And as our daughter came to recognize the myth of Santa Claus and the Easter Bunny, we made her lie to her brother so he wouldn't be disappointed, until he figures out on his own that his parents have orchestrated an enormous charade for years! Can you tell it still bugs me? And, I love Santa Claus. Who doesn't want to believe in a kind, elderly gentleman who loves us enough (if we're good) to squeeze himself down a chimney and leave presents under our Christmas trees?

So here is the point, I know Santa Claus isn't real and yet I still love him. I was programmed from the time I was born until I realized at about age eight that it was my mom and dad sneaking into my room with a stocking stuffed with presents and hanging it on my bedpost. I was wildly excited to find that on Christmas morning. I sincerely disappointed when I realized Santa wasn't real.

Here is some other programming I received during those young years of believing everything I heard and saw with regards to money. My uncles and aunts often referred to people who had more money than them as "rich bastards." Once when I was about age five, I overheard one of my aunts talking about me to someone else. She felt sorry for me because we didn't have much money. Up until then I had been perfectly happy and wasn't aware that we didn't have much money (whatever that means to a five-year-old).

Think of how conflicting my beliefs about money are forming at such a young age. On the one hand, I've been informed that rich people are bastards. Bastards are bad. I know because I'm not allowed to say that word. I've also learned that I am to be pitied because I don't have much money. Does that mean my aunt is a rich bastard? Am I good because I'm poor?

All of this and oh, so much more, is poured into my subconscious mind by the time I'm six years old. "Money doesn't grow on trees," "You don't deserve that," "We can't afford that," "We'll never be rich," and so on.

Take a few moments now to jot down in your journal some of the phrases and ideologies that were poured into your subconscious mind. Acknowledging them is the first step to managing them!

Ego and Soul

Honestly, sometimes I get really fed up of my subconscious—it's like it's got a mind of its own.
—Alexei Sayle

Our current reality is created by our subconscious beliefs and conditioning from our past. That subconscious programming overrides the "Thoughts Become Things" philosophy. Just like our computer is not the operating system (OS) that runs it, it is merely the container for the operating system.

This is my philosophy. Humans have two operating systems. Our Ego is the container for our subconscious belief system that operates from past conditioning and experience (not all of it is bad). Our Soul is the creative operating system that believes in our dreams and desires. Our bodies are the containers for both our Egos and our Souls. Once we become aware of both belief systems, we can utilize our free will and choice as to which OS to run.

To manifest the business and lifestyle our Souls are yearning to experience, we must first recognize and acknowledge the lower vibration of the subconscious default operating system, before we can shift to the higher vibration of our Souls. The vibration that matches what we are intentionally calling into our lives.

You will know which operating system you are in alignment with based on the results you experience in your life.

Not Quantum Leap Ready

> *I do a weird thing when I am nervous where I tilt*
> *my head back like I am super confident. This is my*
> *attempt to fake it until I make it, or at the very*
> *least make it easier for someone to slit my throat.*
> —**Amy Poehler**, *Yes Please*

Here's another phrase I'm sure you are familiar with, *Fake It Till You Make It!* There are many examples of people who have pretended to be successful until they actually became successful. The way to know if they were truly in alignment with a successful belief system is if they sustained their success!

My grand attempt to fake it until I made it ended in ego-crushing ashes. I learned all the tools and practices of the trade, dressed for success, and emulated the superstars. I had my vision board on the wall and affirmations on my bathroom mirror. I loved the coaching, working with the horses, and especially hosting retreats with horses! I brought in over $100,000 in the first 18 months of launching my own business. Pretty effin' amazing for someone who had been a stay at home mom for the previous nine years. I should have been celebrating my success and jumping for joy. But I wasn't. I was disappointed because it didn't happen in 12 months, and I was embarrassed because I had $20,000 worth of debt as a result of all the training and infrastructure involved. Because I didn't know what I didn't know at the time, I also had not properly set up financial cash flow and investments. And, the biggest, ugliest reason for the crash of my first attempt at "success" was my unconscious Ego operating system. I hadn't been aware of the fact that in matters of money, it wasn't my positive affirmations running the show.

My Soul had big plans and very much wanted to bring those plans to fruition. Unfortunately, I was not spiritually or mentally prepared to sustain the quantum leap I was attempting. The predominant belief system driving my results was based on the fear of being discovered as a fake... Who did I think I was to hit a goal like that? I didn't have any experience with earning my own wealth. Who was I to help others build a successful business? My early childhood programming reminded me that rich people are bastards, wealth is for other people, I'm not educated enough, someone else does it better than me, and on and on and on ... crash. Game over.

It's the Truth, Until It's Not

Truth is a pathless land.
—**Krishnamurti**

We associate the word "truth" with "fact." Our collective agreement is that truth is immovable; it's a constant "what is." Our alignment with the Truth is how we come to make sense of the world, define our role as citizens, organize ourselves as societies, and create rules and laws to protect us from harm.

But what is your personal truth? Has your truth evolved and changed over the years or is it permanently fixed and immovable? You might be surprised to hear me say that either way, that's the truth. That is your truth, today.

Consider the 'facts' of our past that were held as immutable truths that are no longer true (or shouldn't be) today.

- The world is flat.
- The sun revolves around the earth.
- Civilization began 5000 years ago.
- Eating fat will make you fat.
- You will burn in hell if you eat meat on Friday.
- You will burn in hell if you don't accept my God as your God (sorry anyone who still believes this).
- Animals don't have Souls.
- Races should be segregated.
- Males are superior to females.

When we speak and act from our Souls' authentic truth, we are empowered and in alignment with our highest potential. We are connected to God Consciousness (consciousness for the greater Good). We have the tools and ability to access and embrace this consciousness every moment of every day regardless of our religious, ethnic, or political background. We do not have to be ordained, crowned or elected' to receive and allow the truth to flow through our conscious awareness. What we do have to be is *awake*.

Money and Soul

> *Once we believe in ourselves, we can risk*
> *curiosity, wonder, spontaneous delight, or any*
> *experience that reveals the human spirit.*
> **—e. e. cummings**

People who are awake question everything through a curious lens. They recognize that everything is possible, and there are many truths. They know that every human system of development, religion, politics, economics, and education is built on a rigid belief system: a belief that if the system worked before it will always work this way.

Many people are now waking up and realizing the assumptions they have about money or politics or a relationship or anything, may no longer be true. It is confusing and emotionally challenging to confront past conditioning: to acknowledge that most of your life assumptions and beliefs in what is right and righteous may be completely invalid.

Maybe you've been awake for some time now, but have not yet integrated your new awareness into a new structure for aligning with the income and sustainability you require to bring your work with the horses to more people. Many people have a visceral dislike for the "money stuff" associated with doing business. If this is you, please do not hate me for what I'm about to say.

Money is an integral part of our spiritual growth and collective healing. That means money is an integral part of your individual spiritual growth and healing.

If we want our relationship with money to be less "icky," then we need to pay attention to our underlying beliefs and behavior to how money has been coming and going in our life up until now.

We're going to take a deeper dive into this topic in the next chapter.

Take a breath here to ask yourself this question, *What assumptions have I been operating on with regards to the value of my service?*

I need more experience before I can charge for my service.

The people I want to serve can't afford much.

I have to offer a lot more service to charge more money.

People will think I'm greedy or think too much of myself.

What other thoughts have you been having about money with regards to your business? Take a moment to write them down in your journal.

I can't count how many times I've heard a practitioner say, "I wish I didn't have to charge money. I wish I could just do it for free and not worry about money." You can! Go ahead and offer your programs and services for free. If you're not bringing in clients anyway who are paying you, then you are not giving up existing income by giving your service for free.

However, you will be giving up the energy of your time and resources, and the time and energy of your horses, who need to eat too! And most importantly, you will be giving away the credibility of the entire equine assisted learning industry.

If you decide to go that route, and give your services away for free, please write to me and let me know how fulfilled you are after six months. That is, if anyone shows up. The people you want to serve still need to be able to find you.

And if you are someone who can afford to give your services away for free, it's likely that the person you are hoping to serve would not value the experience to its full potential. Because in our society's collective belief system—the perception of value is determined by investment.

If the population you wish to serve cannot pay you because of their socio-economic conditions, there are non-profit organizations set up to serve those populations that will pay for your service. You might launch your own non-profit organization to serve those people. It still requires money to flow in your direction, no matter how you label it.

Transitioning from our default ego-orientated operating system to our creative soul-based operating system can be harder than you would think. Our Ego is convinced that it has the facts and figures all worked out. It likes rigid structures that don't change. On the flip side, your Soul craves variety and expansion. Your Soul has no problem expressing the value of who you are and what you offer. Your Soul celebrates reciprocal appreciation.

If your perfect client walked up to you today and said, "I really want to work with you. How much should I make the check out for?" What would you say?

Interest follows investment.
—**Sandra Scherer** (wise friend)

 Lesson: Money and Ego
Access Link: https://schelliwhitehouse.com/bch/

Why You Should Do This Exercise...
Excavating your deeply rooted beliefs and behaviors around money is the first step to creating a new relationship with abundance. Awareness is the first step. Action is a better step!

Chapter Eight

YOUR SPIRITUAL MONEY MIRROR

*Don't tell me where your priorities are. Show me where
you spend your money and I'll tell you what they are.*
—James W. Frick

How You Do Money Is How You Do Anything

As you know by now, I am a soulful entrepreneur. My spiritual growth
is intimately entwined with who I am, what I do, and whom I serve.
In preparation for this section of the book, I spent several months
interviewing people on the subject of spirituality. Out of 33 questions
there was only one direct question about money. Question #28: *How
does money factor on your spiritual path?* I'll get to the insight that
question revealed in a moment. The real eye-opener was question #17:

Do you ever feel stuck on your personal and spiritual journey? Ninety-five percent of the interviewees brought up money as a sticking point on their spiritual path. I find that interesting because, up until that point, there was no conversation about money at all.

When we got to question #28: *How does money factor on your spiritual path?* –the responses fell into these main categories:

Never thought about it.

It's not part of my spiritual path.

I struggle with money and what it represents.

Money is totally integrated within my process of spiritual development.

Can you guess which of the respondents have thriving businesses? I'll give you a hint. It's not the ones who never thought about money as a factor in their personal and spiritual development!

Reflections of Money in History

> *Capital as such is not evil; it is its wrong use that is evil.*
> *Capital in some form or another will always be needed.*
> **—Gandhi**

If we are to create any kind of substantial balance and abundance in our work/life, then we absolutely need to align ourselves with the energy of reciprocity. We give, and we receive in equal measure. As a society, money is a reflection of our collective agreement about its level of usefulness. It is a concept made up as a system of exchanging goods and services. Money has no value without the beliefs we attach to it. Let's take a trip back in time, and see how our evolutionary beliefs around money have become deeply intertwined with our spiritual evolution and our inherent beliefs about what is good and righteous (or not).

Our deep seated societal beliefs about money stem all the way back to our earliest recorded history. Other than the Bible's telling of the

Good Samaritan there are only a handful of stories about people of wealth reaching out to help someone in need, much less influencing the masses, with their wealth, for the greater good. When you bring the history of money (in our society) into perspective it will help you to understand why many of us behave in such a schizophrenic manner over matters of money.

Until very recent history it was nearly impossible for anyone not born into wealth to achieve much more than their hereditary station in life would provide. Over the past several thousand years we have been conditioned to associate monetary wealth with greed, avarice and corruption. This stereotype is portrayed in nearly every movie we've ever watched. Poor people are good, rich people are evil. Who wants to be considered as evil? Certainly, no-one that wants to be known as a soulful do-gooder! I mean that with complete and total respect as that is exactly how I want to be known!

It has only been within the past 250 years where we have experienced an acceleration of individuals creating their own independent wealth outside of inheritance or internal promotion. This is a new wealth stemming from the creative genius of individuals who are open to see a need in their communities and find a way to fill it.

Even more recently for women, it has only been 177 years since we were granted the right to own property. We didn't officially enter the workforce until the 1920's (less than 100 years ago!). Today we are ushering in an era where our own unique expression of service is honored and sought after. We can celebrate a new order of transparency and collaboration. Well, at least that's the new ideal. Yes, we have made leaps and bounds, and if we are to continue to grow into a more collaborative, socially caring society, we need to pay attention to our everyday behavior and mindset with regards to money in order to see a lasting shift toward the recalibration of our collective money consciousness.

The Mirror of Shame

> *Wealth is the ability to fully experience life.*
> —**Henry David Thoreau**

There is a whole organization called Underearners Anonymous. It's a twelve-step program for people who are addicted to earning less than they are worth. Let me repeat that. They are *addicted* to earning less than they are worth! Here are symptoms of the Underearner addiction taken directly from their website:

Symptoms of Underearning

1. **Time Indifference**—We put off what must be done and do not use our time to support our own vision and further our own goals.
2. **Idea Deflection**—We compulsively reject ideas that could expand our lives or careers, and increase our profitability.
3. **Compulsive Need to Prove**—Although we have demonstrated competence in our jobs or business, we are driven by a need to re-prove our worth and value.
4. **Clinging to Useless Possessions**—We hold on to possessions that no longer serve our needs, such as threadbare clothing or broken appliances.
5. **Exertion/Exhaustion**—We habitually overwork, become exhausted, then under-work or cease work completely.
6. **Giving Away Our Time**—We compulsively volunteer for various causes, or give away our services without charge, when there is no clear benefit.
7. **Undervaluing and Under-pricing**—We undervalue our abilities and services and fear asking for increases in compensation or for what the market will bear.

8. **Isolation**—We choose to work alone when it might serve us much better to have co-workers, associates, or employees.

9. **Physical Ailments**—Sometimes, out of fear of being larger or exposed, we experience physical ailments.

10. **Misplaced Guilt or Shame**—We feel uneasy when asking for or being given what we need or what we are owed.

11. **Not Following Up**—We do not follow up on opportunities, leads, or jobs that could be profitable. We begin many projects and tasks but often do not complete them.

12. **Stability Boredom**—We create unnecessary conflict with co-workers, supervisors and clients, generating problems that result in financial distress.

Did you see yourself in any of those above statements? If you did, you're obviously not alone! That's some powerful social proof that there is an epidemic of people who are not living their full potential and consequently may not be capable of taking care of themselves in a healthy manner, much less contribute to the benefit of others.

It's not that these people don't want to have healthy, meaningful work that is also financially rewarding. It's that they have locked themselves into certain patterns of belief that keep them repeating the same actions and behaviors around business and career that keep them stuck in low paying, ungratifying work.

For many heart-centered entrepreneurs I work with, their biggest fear is that they are not worthy of the income they could receive by capitalizing on their own gifts and talents. Yes, it can be scary and growth is sometimes painful—but the rewards are magnificently greater than the toils of the journey. And, it's certainly not a road to travel alone.

Walking a New Spiritual Money Path

> *Let your Soul inform your money*
> *and your money express your Soul.*
> —**Lynne Twist**, *The Soul of Money*

The number of people joining support groups like Underearners Anonymous and other organizations like Debtors Anonymous are proof that progress and healing is far more powerful when you share your fears and victories in a safe, nurturing environment.

We humans are much more likely to break free of limiting and self-sabotaging behavior when we surround ourselves with people who have traveled that path before us and others who are brave enough to travel it now.

Are you ready to boldly go where you've never gone before with your business and your life? Are you ready to toss out what is no longer working (or never worked) and implement what will work to bring in the resources, people, and income you've been fantasizing about?

It takes courage to take a big leap up to the next highest version of the business of your life! A life of enough. Enough for the wellbeing of you, your family, and your herd. Enough for your creative and spiritual growth. Enough to share with your community. Enough to save for the future.

What You See Is What You Get

> *People consciously see what they expect,*
> *rather than what violates their expectations.*
> —**Anil K. Seth**, Editor-in-Chief of *Neuroscience of Consciousness*

If we want our money system to be different in our life and society we must do the hard work and re-wire our personal thinking and mindset first. If we continually expect to be treated unfairly with regards to money because "that's the way it's always been," then we will continue to get ever increasing unfair treatment.

We will not fix our own personal finances with the same thinking, beliefs, and actions that got us here in the first place. One of the well-known fathers of modern coaching, Thomas Leonard said, "How you do one thing is how you do everything." If this is true, we can then assume, *How you do money is how you do everything.*

Some people will totally agree with the first statement, "How you do one thing is how you do everything," then completely disagree with the second, *How you do money is how you do everything.* It's a perfect example of how we have come to compartmentalize money as something separate from our moral and psychic fabric.

The flow of money in your life is directly linked to your thoughts and expectations around money, most of which fall into these four primary mindsets.

Check to see if any of the following statements are true for you:

Acceptability
You believe other people's needs are more important than your own. You often feel responsible for making everything "ok" for others. You can't stand the idea of someone being disappointed with you. To be accepted, you go out of your way to meet the needs of loved ones and co-workers and rarely (if ever) have the time or energy (including finances) to take care of yourself. You haven't learned to say, "No," to others to protect your own well-being. You likely experience a lack of control with money and believe that all the money coming to you is already spent. You often struggle to make ends meet.

Credibility

You believe that what you provide is not valuable or important enough.
This belief can make you feel like a real "push-me-pull-you!" You know
the work you do is transformational for the client, yet your underlying
belief is that you are not important enough to stand out and be seen as
a facilitator of that extraordinary experience. You may hide behind the
mantle of shyness or the introvert label. You invest in your education
and credentials and look to others to validate your importance and value.
You understand the value of investing in yourself, yet struggle with the
value of what you have to offer. You seek security and guarantees and
because there really is no such thing, you feel incongruent offering a
service you technically can't guarantee.

Deservability

You believe that you are not good enough as you are. This is a deep-seated
personal belief that you do not deserve to be compensated for doing
something you love. Especially if it is the work of your heart and Soul,
and you have a natural gift or talent. You have embraced the notion that
work must be hard and ungratifying if it is to be worthy of a meager
allowance of money. You've been taught to give, give, give and to receive
is selfish. If it comes easy to you, it must not be valuable to others. You
may experience burnout and resentment for being undercompensated
and underappreciated.

Love-ability

*You believe people won't accept you if you make more money than they
do.* This belief brings feelings of guilt for having more than others.
If you don't have more, you won't attract it and if you do, you are
likely to lose it very quickly. If you already have wealth, you are likely
to conceal your abundance from the public for fear of being judged
as extravagant or for only being liked because of your money, not

because of who you are. Either way, you like nice things and will often invest in self-care for yourself and others. Even though you are generous, you worry about being taken advantage of or overcharged. You may experience cycles of "feast or famine" with money in your life, as your money-guilt is likely to cause you to undercharge for your services.

You will likely find aspects of yourself in more than one of the four categories. Most of our deep-rooted beliefs and perceptions around money have been handed down to us from family, peers, clergy, and the media. We have been told what to believe and how to behave in a way that is not authentic to our own Soul's purpose. This applies to many, many more circumstances in our lives, but for now, let's stick with money.

Aligned Action

While you pray, move your feet!
—Quaker saying

We have now entered a new place in history with an opportunity to change our relationship with money, to create a new story of beneficial wealth and conscientious abundance through soulful entrepreneurship. Service to others from a place of heart centered giving and receiving.

Our work with the horses has brought the "heart" of our business to the forefront of our priorities. As wonderful as this is, it is also easy to get unbalanced when we spend so much time in our hearts. As an organ of perception our hearts are masters of feeling into what wants to happen next. Unless we engage our intellect to discern the next right action and our gut intelligence to move our feet, we are likely to sit and spin as we congratulate ourselves for being in our hearts, even though nothing is progressing forward in our lives.

I recently attended a course led by Lynne Twist, author of *The Soul of Money* and founder of the Soul of Money Institute. She made a powerful observation with regards to a mindset shift in our society, from regarding ourselves as *citizens* of these United States, to being referred to and primarily labeled as *consumers*. As citizens, we hold ourselves accountable and are contributors to the greater good. As consumers, we are merely expected to devour the greater good.

We have the power to consciously choose a spiritual money path, to create a collaborative, abundant, and resourceful life as citizens of our communities, our country, and our planet, through mindful thoughts and behaviors with regards to how we respond to the financial situations in our everyday environments.

The antidote to the four default money mindsets is to shift from a fear of:

- Not Being Accepted to—A practice of Clear Boundaries: Be generous, yet do not deplete yourself.
- Not Being Credible to—A practice of Demonstrating Your Expertise: Claim yourself as credible.
- Not Being Deserving to—A practice of Receiving Abundance: Courage to demand what you deserve from the Universe!
- Not Being Loveable to—A practice of Loving: Help others see their own value through your eyes.

Reflections of Money and Love

... for where your treasure is, there your heart will be also.
—*Matthew 6: 21*

Finally, and this is a big one.... Love money as a representational vibration of yourself. We know money is a representational currency our society uses for the exchange of goods and services. What currency are you vibrating at? Love is the highest vibrational currency available to us humans. Where is your heart/love with regards to money? Is it for the greater good of all? Can you receive without judgment and allow others to receive as well? If your heart holds fear and resentment around money, then your treasure will also be filled with fear and resentment.

When we take the time to practice love in all things, even and especially toward money, we can then celebrate a new age of abundance and collaboration. Whether you are conscious of it or not, money is a reflection of your deepest beliefs and most definitely a factor on your spiritual path.

> *You have to own that you can give s*
> *omeone a million-dollar minute!*
> —**June Gunter**, TeachingHorse, *Rediscovering Leadership*

 Lesson: Money and Soul
Access Link: https://schelliwhitehouse.com/bch/

Why You Should Do This Exercise...
This is an opportunity to enter into a healing relationship with money and invite it into your business with intention. Give it a positive role to help you grow and serve with purpose.

Chapter Nine

THE HEAD, HEART, AND GUT OF MONEY

For the economy is little more than a barometer
that registers the highs and lows of consciousness.
—Eric **Butterworth**, *Spiritual Economics*

Alignment with Money

Remember, this entire book is structured to integrate our three brain centers, Head, Heart, and Gut. Our relationship with money is no different than any other relationship we work to understand, know intimately, and consciously nurture. Yet the money conversation is so sensitive to most people that they never bring sufficient awareness to their relationship with money so that it can be understood, healed, and consciously nurtured.

In his book, *Money, Master the Game*, Tony Robbins discusses that true mastery with money requires three levels and goes on to list them as: Cognitive Understanding, Emotional Mastery, and Physical Mastery. He then adds, "Repetition is the mother skill".

He just described the Head, Heart, and Gut and added "repetition," which I wholeheartedly agree with.

I'm sure Mr. Tony Robbins would agree with me here if I add that "right repetition" leads to mastery with money.

I did a lot of horsemanship skill building with the Parelli program over the years. Pat Parelli often said, "Practice does not produce perfection. Perfect practice does." Meaning, if you are practicing (repeating) the wrong activity, you will never get the results you desire. When communicating with your horses, they require clear intention, emotional integrity, and aligned action. They become willing partners when they can trust that alignment in you every time you show up. And when you show up out of alignment, they will remind you by their behavior that you are not fully present. They will not perform as before, or they may disengage and walk away. The point is, you don't get a hall pass because you were being present and aware with your horse yesterday and get to "check out" today, or ever. The same is true with how you relate to your finances. If you are not 100% in your body and aligned, Head, Heart, and Gut, then you are no longer the leader. Period.

Horses Read Your Energy, Not Your Resume

> *Talent is always conscious of its own abundance,*
> *and does not object to sharing.*
> **—Aleksandr Solzhenitsyn**

Horses do not care if you have the entire alphabet of credentials behind your name. They do not care about your age, sex, race, religion, socioeconomic status, health, job title, or how much money you do or don't have in the bank. They only respond to who shows up in the moment with them.

Money shows up the same way. I am quite aware that money is not a living, breathing, sentient being. I also believe that your energy towards money behaves in direct response to your relationship with it. You are either aligned and the leader of it, or it "walks away."

In Chapter Seven, we explored our cultural beliefs around money. In Chapter Eight, we examined our emotional relationship with money. In this chapter, we're going to look at some simple, positive behaviors to reinforce the new neural pathways we are developing to be more reciprocal and less fearful with money in our life.

When I first started in this business I was shocked by the competitive push back I witnessed and experienced from some coaches and practitioners. I took on that energy and belief myself for the first couple of years, which as you know, ended in disaster. It was easy for me to align with that thinking because I had not developed a solid foundation in my relationship with money. At the time, for me, money was not just a tool for expanding my soul's purpose, it was the measure of my success and therefore the measure of my credibility.

When I believed that the amount of money I made wasn't enough, and I was no longer credible or deserving, the Universe said, *I feel you, sister,* and took away all that I had and more. The Universe could only respond according to the energy of my belief system. That's not what I wanted at all! The paradox is, what I wanted and what I "believed" were not the same thing. Therefore, my actions had no lasting effect.

Prepare Your Container

If you're not ready to receive, you won't be able to sustain your wealth.
—Angela Lauria, *The Difference*

The competitive mindset breeds fear and discontent with regards to money. It creates a container based on a belief that there is not enough for all and that someone must do without. If your mindset is world-wide competition for a finite amount of money, then you will find yourself in a constant state of judging if you deserve what you have, or whether someone else deserves what they have. Competition for wealth or status is steeped in false self and ego driven beliefs. If you believe in "not enough," then you will experience "not enough."

There are 7 billion people on this planet, and more are born every day! What percentage of those people can you possibly serve in your lifetime? Even if you had 100 people a week come to work with the horses, 52 weeks per year for the next 30 years, that's only 156,000 people.

There is no competition. There is only you, doing what you do best for the people you are meant to serve. It doesn't matter if there are 20 other equine assisted practitioners in your county. You have a unique gift to serve a unique group of people, just as the others do. Stand in your integrity and desire to serve for the highest good of all.

With the same integrity, create your container for receiving that which you ask for. This means you need to pay attention to your business the same way you pay attention to the well-being of your family and your horses.

Conscious Giving and Gaining

If we command our wealth, we shall be rich and free.
If our wealth commands us, we are poor indeed.
—Edmund Burke

How many times have you heard someone say, "There is infinite abundance and plenty for everyone!" I desperately wanted to believe that, but often found it hard to resonate with that sentiment when there were so many others going without having their basic needs met. I came to realize that a good barometer for measuring my own belief system with money was to notice how I responded to the plight of others.

Imagine you drive up to a stop light, and there is someone panhandling. Do you roll down your window and hand them some money?

Do you look the other way because you feel uncomfortable?

Do you judge whether they are worthy of your donation based on how they are dressed or some 'vibe' you pick up?

Are you more likely to give to a woman versus a man?

What if they have a child with them or a dog?

What if the same person is on the same corner several days in a row? Do you give something every day?

Do you feel resentful because you gave yesterday?

Do you plan ahead and bring them a bagel and coffee?

What if you notice they have on a new pair of shoes and a new jacket? Do they still get the bagel and coffee or are they cut off now because they moved up in appearance?

If they are able bodied do you offer them work in exchange for more money?

What if they told you (if you happened to ask) that they had a job at Walmart, but couldn't make ends meet and found they could make more money begging from strangers while standing in every kind of weather day in and day out.

Would you still give them money even though you knew they could get a job?

You remember the phrase from Thomas Leonard in Chapter Eight, "How you do one thing is how you do everything." How you respond to the panhandler is also a reflection of how you do money.

If you feel guilty because you are in a nice, warm car and she is standing in the cold wind, then you struggle with deserve-ability.

If you judge whether the beggar is worthy of your donation based on an assumption of the value of the clothes they are wearing or other attributes, you may equate your own value with credibility.

If you give her your last $20 and can't put gas in your car to get to work the next day, you have serious issues with acceptability.

If your concern is how the panhandler might judge you as someone who "has" when he "has not," then you are wrestling with lovability.

The Gift

The greatest gift that you can give to others is
the gift of unconditional love and acceptance.
—**Brian Tracy**

Last winter there was a man who showed up on a corner that I drive past several times a week at various times of the day. He was a veteran and looked like he'd had some pretty rough times in his past. I don't remember if I gave him anything the first time I saw him (the light might have been green), but I did offer something several times over the next couple of months. He made that corner his regular gig. Honestly, I went through every single one of those emotional responses I just listed. There were days I chose a different route so I wouldn't have to deal with him being there. Some days, I resented the fact I would have to drive past him. Other days I planned for the encounter and had a couple bucks ready in case I got caught at the light.

One day as I was journaling about my own judgments around money, and why I was struggling to move to the next level of wealth accumulation, it dawned on me that this man was a gift. A message from the Universe to notice and appreciate all that I have: all the abundance and love and great work I get to experience. I am not the one spending my days on a street corner and depending on the mercy of strangers.

My resentment of him shifted to a feeling of love and appreciation. I was giddy with this revelation! I wholly appreciated his journey in this life. I no longer pitied him. I honored his process and his experience as uniquely his own. I *respected* his right to be exactly who he is, a human being doing the best he can with who he is today. If I feel anxious, guilty, scared, or generous because of his presence, that is all on me. He is simply getting by to the best of his ability.

I got in the car and drove to his corner with $20 in my pocket. I wanted to make his day! A policeman pulled in front of me and as I approached my new friend (who didn't know he was my friend now), his flashers came on. My heart stopped. The man put his sign down. *Oh, no!* I thought he was being arrested. Then the most beautiful scene took place. The policeman got out of the car with a bag of food and a drink from Chick-fil-A (which was across the street) and took it to my friend. He shook his hand and got back in the car. The light turned green, and I had to move with the traffic. I could see the delight on the man's face as he held the gift in his hands. I thought my heart would explode. The policeman and I had the very same thought and impetus to act towards this man at the same time. I don't know what the policeman's motivation was but mine was pure gratitude. And I was overjoyed to see the cop respond with such kindness and respect.

I did my errands and drove back around the block so I could give him the $20 I had intended. He wasn't there. He's never been back. I get teary every time I share this story. It was as if the Universe said to me, *You got it! Time to move on.*

As I became conscious of my giving and accepted all that is, even the bits I perceived as uncomfortable, I was able to access a deep well of gratitude that until that point had been a weak trickle. A trickle that went something like, *I appreciate this, but that would be better.* My gratitude was conditional. When I wasn't experiencing the world exactly as I'd wanted it, my appreciation for what is and what is available was fairly anemic. It still takes practice and vigilance to keep the waters flowing, but now the pity party may only last minutes instead of the days, months, and even years that I used to endure.

Can You Be Grateful for What You Have Not Got?

A simple shift in attitude can help us recognize the
hidden potential for fulfillment in every event.
—Madisyn Taylor

Money loves to be paid attention to, like a young puppy. If you're not paying attention, he will wander off and maybe even get lost (aack, I don't even want to visit the rest of that scenario). The best way to pay attention to money is to keep it occupied, just like a puppy. Give it a job to do, or several!

I like to plan out the responsibilities for my money. Especially on days when I'm feeling in harmony and alignment with life. The money I already have, and the money that's winging its way to my bank account as needed.

This requires a special kind of gratitude attitude, the ability to be grateful for what you have not gotten (yet).

The Universe abhors a vacuum. If you create a 'container' for a need or desire to be fulfilled, the Universe will fill that container to overflowing, if you pay attention to it!

Sounds silly, right? How can you be thankful for the extra $1000.00 in the bank when you see nothing there?

Let me explain. When someone pays you a compliment, buys you a gift, or simply holds a door open for you—your response is "Thank You." It's an immediate response to an act of generosity. Everyone understands this.

Now think of a time you confided your relationship woes to a friend, "he/she doesn't understand me, we just aren't connecting, he/she never listens, I don't know how to get his/her attention", etc., etc.

You have not only confided your woes to a friend but you have *affirmed* to the Universe that your relationship is miserable. Now what happens? You get *more* of what you affirm for yourself.

If you look at your bank account as the fixed budget or income you have to live on, then you are affirming to the Universe this is all you want. By creating specific "containers" for what you intend to manifest, you tell the Universe to get busy arranging the details!

A container can be separate saving accounts, an investment account, or a simple ledger. It could even be a big white board on your wall where you track the amount you accumulate in each container every month! Make it fun. Make it interactive. Make it real.

If you sincerely want help (with anything), you must stop focusing on any negative aspect of the situation. That doesn't mean you deny "what is," it means that you must take your focus off of what you *don't* want and direct it toward what you *do* want and create the space for its inevitable arrival with deep and profound *gratitude*.

What if You Knew It Was Coming?

Abundance is a process of letting go;
that which is empty can receive.
—Bryant H. McGill

Imagine you are in between jobs, and before you start the new job you come up short on funds and are unable to pay your heating bill. It's the middle of winter, and you've received a notice that your heat will be turned off if full payment isn't received in three days' time.

First you panic and sling a few choice expletives around the room. Next, you take action, call a friend or relative, and beg or borrow enough money to pay your heating bill.

For the sake of this scenario, let's say your friend says, "Sure, you can pick up a check tomorrow." You gush with gratitude, promise to pay them back, and breathe a sigh of relief. Then you forget about that problem because it has been solved.

When you hang up the phone with your friend you are filled with gratitude for the assistance they have offered, correct? Even though you do not have that money in your possession you are already grateful for it. You know it is coming, but you have not *gotten* it yet.

This is exactly the way we need to establish our relationship with Our Infinite Source of Power. Our relationship with Source is exactly the same. Once you ask for help, gush with gratitude for what you have requested and know that it is most definitely on its way. Then stop worrying about what you haven't got.

I'm sure you are familiar with the Law of Cause and Effect. For every action, there is always an equal and opposite reaction. Therefore, your *grateful* outreaching to Universal Source creates an instantaneous reaction from Source back to you.

You are now responsible for receiving that which you have requested, and you'd better have a container to put it in! And guess what? It may not show up as cash, yet the result will be the same or better! Let the Universe handle those details.

Whatever we are waiting for—peace of mind,
contentment, grace, the inner awareness of simple
abundance—it will surely come to us, but only when we
are ready to receive it with an open and grateful heart.
—Sarah Ban Breathnach

Lesson: Aligning Service and Price
Access Link: https://schelliwhitehouse.com/bch/

Why You Should Do This Exercise...
You now know who you are, what you are an expert at doing, and whom you want to serve. You have also worked through some sticky money hang-ups that may have been preventing you from receiving the value of what you are worth for many years.

Now it's time to create the programs and service you plan to provide and set the value in a way that supports your efforts and moves your clients forward!

Chapter Ten

ALMOST READY!

*Spectacular achievement is always
preceded by unspectacular preparation.*
—Robert H. Schuller

This chapter is where we bring it all together. You know that you are
the soul of your business, you know what you stand for, and you have
claimed your super power expertise. You have identified the people you
will serve and created a platform to serve them effectively that also serves
you! The final element is to extend the invitation to work with you!

You Are Naturally Creative, Resourceful, and Whole

Show me your original face before you were born.
—Buddhist koan

According to the *Co-Active Coaching Model* one of the cornerstones of a great coach is the ability to hold their clients as naturally creative, resourceful, and whole. It's an incredibly important fundamental skill and the foundation for all possibilities to a successful outcome for the client.

You are at the place where you must hold yourself as naturally creative, resourceful, and whole, in order to invite others into your practice. You've come a long way, gotten your head on straight, checked in with your feelings, and learned to listen to their advice. Now we move into action. Up until now it's been an exploration of possibility and potential.

You are ready to make the leap and stand in the next highest version of your horse and soul business.

The Business of Your Soul

Age wrinkles the body. Quitting wrinkles the soul.
—**Douglas MacArthur**

Before we get to the final element required to align with your ready, willing, and able clients, I want to talk about the 'business of your soul." It is your Soul's business to guide you in this journey of personal evolution. Guess what? Your Soul / Higher Self / Spirit already has all of the answers and knows the quickest way to everything! However, you dear human, are on a journey, a quest to become the best possible human in this allotted lifetime. Think of your soul as your Angel Coach. A good coach does not hand their client immediate solutions, a good coach holds the space for their client to connect with their own super genius abilities and find the solution that works best for this moment. A good coach will never tell you what to do, yet will offer knowledge if it is requested. It's up to you to request the knowledge your soul has to share with you and to listen to the answers.

Most often those answers may come through the sensations and emotions of your body, as well as your mind, which may include abstract thoughts in the form of images, colors, lyrics, or snippets of dialogue.

Remember to check in with your body to notice when you are in alignment with the actions to be taken.

- Learn to understand your body's solid *yes* and solid *no*.
- Acknowledge vulnerability as a barometer of impending change and learn to lean into it.

The bad news is, there will be a lot of feeling vulnerable. It's part of the growth process. The good news is, it gets easier, and the process becomes shorter and shorter with practice and allowance.

Your soul is always standing before you and eager to move forward. It's easy to get caught in the enthusiasm of what's to come. Know that when you become anxious during the execution of the work necessary to grow your business, it is an indication that you need to process and acknowledge the doubts and fears you may still be harboring. Physically processing our doubts and fears is a vital aspect of your growing your business, because it's not all just in your head. Your past experiences are coded into your cellular memory. You are rebuilding new cellular neural pathways by your new beliefs and actions, but your body may not always respond according to your best interest.

Your new image is one of confidence, self-worth, compassion, and success. You know it, your Soul knows it (is it), and now your clients know it. Your body may not fully know it yet.

E-L-E-F-A-N-T

If you have the guts to keep making mistakes, your wisdom
and intelligence leap forward with huge momentum.
—Holly Near

Second grade was the end of my championship career. I won the joggle contest in my class that year by swinging a ball on a rope around my ankle 502 times! In the third grade, I was in the championship spelling bee (for my class). The whole grade school was assembled in the gymnasium, and it was down to my arch nemesis, Susie Hershberger, and me. The word was ELEPHANT and I went first. E-L-E-F.... As soon as I said the letter F out loud, I knew I blew it. I stopped and choked, and Susie spelled it perfectly. I was crushed. I wish I could say that little event wasn't important. Obviously was, or I wouldn't still remember it so vividly. I was embarrassed by that silly mistake. Embarrassed to the core of my nine-year-old heart to the point I no longer trusted myself to be the best at anything.

I repeatedly came in second and third in most of the school competitions all the way through ninth grade, then gave up sports and competitions all together. That mindset was ingrained in my everything. I know I have great leadership qualities and am often way ahead of most situations, but I was never *the* leader and if I was, it didn't last for very long. I got used to being second. It actually became comfortable because then I wasn't the one responsible for the outcome.

That was a big, huge awareness for me that unlocked a pattern of behavior that had served me well over the years. It had also kept me small. It's almost laughable to think about the impact that one embarrassing moment had on my whole life. My mind and my soul know that mistakes are for learning and preparing us for the next experience, so we can do things differently. But my body and ego held that belief to be true no matter what. It took some time to reset my physical responses to perceived events of failure and rejection, so I didn't crawl under my self-pity blanket and stop trying.

Working with the horses helped me to recognize first, embrace second, and then finally embody my own leadership capability. That doesn't mean crap doesn't still come up for me. It does.

Your crap is going to come up too. Especially if you've never run a successful business before, and you are now the leader of your own company. You must let it out, and keep a muck bucket nearby.

If I Only Had a Brain

> *I don't know... but some people without*
> *brains do an awful lot of talking... don't they?*
> —**Scarecrow**, *The Wizard of Oz*

I used to die inside at the prospect of having to talk to someone about the work I do, if I perceived them to be smarter than me. For too many years, one of the ways I invalidated myself, my insights, and innovative ideas was by hiding behind the belief that I wasn't credible because I never went to college. Even though I have been a lifelong learner and completed numerous trainings and have the equivalent of a PhD from the "School of Hard Knocks," I never had the college experience and never earned the degree.

Like the scarecrow from *The Wizard of Oz*, I yearned for a declaration from outside of myself to tell me that I was good enough, qualified, and credible. Because this was the lens of how I perceived myself in the world, I frequently did not share the power of my unique brilliance, for fear of not being taken seriously. I often missed opportunities to contribute an important insight that could improve, not only the circumstances of my own life, but of those I shared my life with!

Gorgeous opportunities came galloping by, and I marveled at their existence as I watched them sail past me. There have been a few times I tried to grab onto a handful of flying mane and pull myself up. I would get a few miles down the path and ready to leap over the first obstacle when my wicked false self would yell, *What the hell are you doing? You're not qualified to make that jump!* Then he'd grab me and throw me to the ground to save me from myself and the leap I was about to make.

Numerous people never got to experience the transformational benefit of the work I offer through coaching with horses, because I assumed that they would believe I wasn't credible enough to help them.

Because of my own insecurity, I didn't invite them to work with me. I made the decision for them and denied them a magnificent opportunity to experience themselves in a way they may have never imagined.

Truth and Tell

The greatest good you can do for another is not just
to share your riches but to reveal to him his own.
—Benjamin Disraeli

In honor of transparency I will confess that I still wish (not as fervently as I used to) that I had a degree. And not just a degree, I want a PhD. But I no longer want it because I need other people to approve of me. I want it because I love to learn and deeply study whatever I'm interested in. I would like to have a PhD in philosophy and metaphysics. Because the process of acquiring that degree would be the result of sitting with professors and scholars and to study how great thinkers think and then apply it to real life. And then I would teach them about the wisdom of horses and get them out of their heads and into their bodies! So, that's my little fantasy, and although I know it is possible to do that in my lifetime, it is not probable. I could start as a college freshman and spend the next five to seven years working on a degree. It would cost between $120,000 to $250,000 (that's in-state tuition), and would not add one dime of earning power to my present potential.

I share this example from my life to illustrate that whatever is holding you back from fully stepping into a profitable and sustainable business needs to be acknowledged and accepted for what it is. Pretending it's not there or that it doesn't matter is a set-up for a fall off that gorgeous horse of opportunity. And when you can accept yourself as you are, the good, the bad, and the beautiful, you give your clients permission to do the same.

The Universe and I Are One

Practicing qigong is so simple and so powerful. You cannot do it wrong. You can only do it good, better, or best.
—Chunyi Lin

Inviting people to step into a valuable program of transformation is a big commitment for the client and an awesome responsibility for you. I know you are comfortable with your ability to coach and facilitate your client from where they are today to where they want to be. However, if you are struggling with enrollment, you may not be showing up powerfully in the invitation to work with you. Your invitation is the first part of the delivery of your service and program. It's where you genuinely get to know your potential client and discover if they are meant to be served by you. This powerful conversation deserves mindful attention and practice.

During my coach training I learned a mindfulness practice called 'Qigong'. Qi means "energy" and Gong means "to work with." Simply put, Qigong means working with the body's energy. We were introduced to the Spring Forest form of Qigong created by Master Chunyi Lin. I bought a home study course from the website and began to practice on my own.

Master Chunyi Lin suggests that as we move through the routine of the exercises that we incorporate a mantra along with our breath that goes like this: breathe in, *I am in the Universe,* breathe out, *The Universe is in me,* breathe in, *The Universe and I are One.* Repeat throughout the rest of the routine. The mantra, the movement, and the breath become a moving meditation and a means of aligning our mind, body, and soul into one breathing entity in harmony and motion.

I was not very coordinated or syncopated with my breath, thoughts, and movement when I began this practice. It is a practice. An evolution of awareness and fluidity between head and heart that becomes actualized in the body until the body owns it on a cellular level, and even then, practice is required for maintenance and to build a solid platform for excellence.

This exercise is taught as a tool for preparing ourselves to be in the presence of the horse and our clients. When we know what alignment feels like, we can better recognize when we are not in alignment. Our horses will also show us when we are not in alignment when we are in their presence. However, the clearer we are before we engage with the horse and client, the purer the experience for the client.

This is how you want to be when you enter into a conversation with someone about the possibility of working with you. When you are fully present with your potential client and able to ask powerful questions, all of your conversations will always be good, better, or best!

A real conversation always contains an invitation. You are
inviting another person to reveal herself or himself to you, to tell
you who they are or what they want.
—David Whyte

Lesson: The Invitation
Access Link: https://schelliwhitehouse.com/bch/

Why You Should Do This Exercise...

Every ideal client that you don't invite to work with you will either continue to suffer with the problem you can most definitely help them with, or they will find someone else to help to them. This is the heart-to-heart conversation where you and your ideal client choose to dance forward together or you guide them to another resource that is a better fit for them at this time. Making this conversation your own will change the quality of your business forever.

Chris Irwin

From equestrian training to executive coaching, mentoring for disadvantaged youth, resiliency workshops for 1st Responders and Military Veterans, to therapeutic, wellness programs, and even the prison system, the scope and impact of Irwin Insights are reaching far beyond the horse industry. As the *Toronto Star* wrote: "Chris Irwin is a man on a mission—to change the way we communicate with each other; one horse at a time." Author of *Horses Don't Lie* and *Dancing with Your Dark Horse.*

Q: *What is the biggest challenge you see in our industry right now?*

Chris: "I see too many wounded healers doing more harm than good. People with great hearts and a wish to help are setting up programs for people who have experienced intense trauma. Some of these people have no experience with the trauma these people have endured or they haven't dealt with their own deep trauma and are not psychologically fit to work with that population. I'm also concerned with the trend of unskilled practitioners rescuing abused horses when they haven't done their own deep work, often they both become more damaged."

Q: *What advice do you have for a new practitioner?*

Chris: "Develop your work in small steps. There is a balance between altruism and practicality. I have been humbled and overwhelmed by the grace of this work. Still, it requires practical business sense, and there is money involved. Build a business that facilitates meaningful change and gets results, and the right people will find you."

Dr. Jenn Oikle

After getting her PhD in clinical psychology, with a specialty in love and relationships, Dr. Jenn was introduced to the emerging field of Healing with Horses.

Chapter Eleven

EXPERT ADVICE

Practice isn't the thing you do once you're good.
It's the thing you do that makes you good.
—**Malcolm Gladwell**, *Outliers: The Story of Success*

Words of Wisdom

As research for this book I interviewed several of our industry experts. These are individuals who have been pioneers in equine assisted therapy, coaching, and leadership development for as long as 30 years! They have worked diligently as both advocates for the horse and the development of human potential.

I asked many questions about their start in the industry and how they came to embrace their various approaches and connect with the population they now serve. But the two questions that got the most energized responses were, One: "What is the biggest challenge you see in our industry right now?" and Two: "What advice do you have for a new practitioner?"

I share their responses here, in alphabetical order as well as their contact information in the resource section at the end of this book. Of course, there are many other amazing, wonderful, qualified teachers and practitioners to learn from in our industry, and I hope to speak to them all one day. However, my publisher has me on a deadline, and I reached as many of our wise leaders as I could!

Alyssa Aubrey

Medicine Horse Ranch/ Alyssa Aubrey is the HorseDream® USA License holder and facilitates HorseDream® Licensed Partner Training Programs for qualified individuals interested in becoming licensed to offer horse assisted leadership programs.

She has developed nationally recognized curriculum that includes best practices and core principles for the field, providing hands on training, coursework, and experiential learning through mentoring and apprenticeship participation at Medicine Horse Ranch.

Alyssa is the co-author of the bestselling book, *The Road to Success* with Jack Canfield. Download a free chapter from her website!

Q: What is the biggest challenge you see in our industry right now?
Alyssa: "Too many practitioners entering this field who haven't done their own deep work. From the years 2000 to 2004 our industry grew 400%. You cannot go through one or two weekends of training and come away with the understanding of what it means to hold the human psyche in one hand and a flight animal in the other! People have forgotten how to learn, to study, and to develop their craft."

Q: What advice do you have for a new practitioner?
Alyssa: "Find a seasoned facilitator and shadow them. Practice the role over and over. Go study broadly. Learn the somatic expression of th client. Do your own deep work first for the safety of everyone concerned Care for the horse, they are not a tool, they take on emotional conten Study horse psychology, behavior and health. Do your own work all th time. You are in a collaborative. None of us know as much as we thin we do. We are the gatekeepers to a sacred trust, we have to protect it.

Angela Dunning
Reclaiming our wildness can play a vital part in the healing of humar and horses. Angela's approach is firmly rooted in the innate wisdor of nature, and in the ancient beliefs of Shamanism. Author of *Th Horse Leads the Way: Honoring the True Role of the Horse in Equir Facilitated Practice*.

Q: What is the biggest challenge you see in our industry right now?
Angela: "I'm both confused and concerned about how horses ar being used and overworked in many practices. The rapidity of growt has resulted in a lack of quality. It's horrifying to me that some get *certification* in a weekend. I am concerned for the clients, the horse and the trainers."

Q: What advice do you have for a new practitioner?
Angela: "Take a breath and go shadow with a more experience practitioner. Don't run before you can walk. Connect with a superviso ASAP, a coach or mentor, and learn how to apply this work into a real life practice. Do your personal work and healing, and learn about th business. Learn about horses in nature and how to properly care fo them in our human environment.

That fateful moment sparked an unexpected spiritual awakening, from which, thankfully, she never recovered! The horses became her healers, allowing her to retrieve her True Self from her own dark night of the soul, a 15-year journey with chronic fatigue syndrome. The horses have become her patient teachers, escorts, and guides into the worlds of Spirit, Animal Communication, Shamanism, and Energy Healing.

Q: What is the biggest challenge you see in our industry right now?
Dr. Jenn: "It's hard to sell services if your intended clients don't know they need what you offer: if they aren't already looking for you! Most people still have no idea what Equine-assisted anything is ... when you mention it, they still have the picture of "therapeutic riding," of disabled kids sitting on horseback. Most people have no other concept available to them. So, they don't see how that's relevant to their own issues or situation.

Creating greater awareness and education of the public about the whole field is the greatest opportunity.

It's extremely hard to sell services when people:

- Don't know what is it
- Don't understand how it works
- Can't see how it will help them
- Have no frame of reference for why they should be seeking that out for their problem

Q: What advice do you have for a new practitioner?
Dr. Jenn: "NICHE NICHE NICHE! Most people finish their programs and create these totally general websites that no one is really going to be interested in because it's too general. It gets back to the original problem...which is that no one is looking for you, for what you have to offer.

"You have to get super specific about whom you want to help and design programming that speaks directly to them, that's going to work for their specific issues.

"You have to think about whom you want to help. Whom exactly can you get passionate about serving? Because in order to find those people, you need to know where they are and how you can connect to them.

"The best niches are ones you are passionate and knowledgeable about AND…

- You can narrow down to real specifics
- You can find where they are, i.e. you can think of ways to connect in with referral partners.
- They have a burning issue and have the money to spend on it.

"You've got to get right down to an important pain point that someone would be willing to spend money to solve or improve."

June Gunter

With 30 years of experience in leadership development, June brings depth of understanding and clarity of purpose to preparing leaders for innovation and transformation. Her specialty is in international equine experiential leadership development for teams and corporate leaders. June holds a Doctor of Education degree in the field of Adult Learning from North Carolina State University. She is a Certified Equine Guided Educator (CEGE), Certified Equine Interaction Professional (CEIP-ED) and the author of *TeachingHorse: Rediscovering Leadership*.

Q: What is the biggest challenge you see in our industry right now?
June: "My experience and focus is on bringing this work to the corporate world. It is a concern to me that there are people who believe that the

corporate industry will invest in a horse facilitated experience without the coaches investing in them. You cannot be content neutral. There are two trends in leadership development that hold a lot of potential. One, corporations are seeking experiential learning, we provide that. Two, the work needs to be customized to the learner. We must be able to demonstrate immediate applicability of the experience to the client's work. An 'aha' is the booby prize. The true added value is the action they will take as a result of what they have learned."

Q: What advice do you have for a new practitioner?
June: "If you want to serve in the corporate world, go live inside an organization. Make connections with local leaders and innovation incubators with the intent of creating relationships and being of service."

Kathleen Barry Ingram

Kathleen brings over 30 years of experience in the counseling field, non-profit services, and marketing and communications in the healthcare industry to her work as a coach and consultant to individuals, families, and businesses.

Kathleen is well known for co-developing and launching the first Epona Equestrian Services apprenticeship class in 2003, with Linda Kohanov. Kathleen and Linda taught the apprenticeship program together until 2007 when the ninth class graduated and another group of talented and experienced individuals began their own equine facilitated learning practices.

Q: What is the biggest challenge you see in our industry right now?
Kathleen: "There are two challenges I see in our industry, specifically for the individual practitioner. One, is that it's hard to define what we do. They don't know what their niche or specialty is in relationship to the work with the horses. The other is, many do not understand

the nuances between coaching and psychotherapy. This can be dangerous."

Q: What advice do you have for a new practitioner?
Kathleen: "Practitioners need support to take the work out into the world, as there is a lot more to learn about the business of this business. My advice is to work with a mentor or coach to anchor the foundational piece of their work, and then bring the horses in."

Lisa Murrell

Lisa is the founder and CEO of Equine Alchemy (2008), the first equine assisted certified coach training program in the world accredited by the ICF (International Coach Federation). Lisa's philosophy is there are three fundamental skills sets to be developed as a competent practitioner of equine assisted coaching.

- professional level coaching skills
- foundational equine facilitation skills
- the ability to integrate the two—it's the integration of these skills that provides a safe space for client transformation

Q: What is the biggest challenge you see in our industry right now?
Lisa: "There's a challenge with getting people to take this work seriously. It comes both from the public not understanding the transformational value and because many practitioners don't understand the value of what they can deliver. Also, there are many certification programs that are not preparing practitioners with the understanding of the systemic work required to integrate their coaching or therapy with the horse. The horse has become a tool in too many programs, which dilutes the integrity of the work."

Q: What advice do you have for a new practitioner?

Lisa: "First, do your own internal work. Know thyself! Be ready for emotional upheaval and transformation. And if you are starting your business, do the important work on your relationship with money! Invest in the same level of coaching and mentoring to build your business as you did in learning your facilitation and coaching skills."

The Kick in the Pants

Just do the work.

—**Linda Kohanov**, *(spoken directly to Schelli Whitehouse)*

Before someone can join my 9-week Business Development course, I require they take an assessment, and then we have an interview to go over the assessment together. Some are disappointed when they learn they are not ready for my program. Although my nature is to see the humor in life and life's challenges, there is nothing humorous about stepping into a professional status as a healer of humans with horses, if you do not thoroughly understand your role or skill level.

At the beginning of Chapter Two, I said my mission is to help equine inspired transformation become the most sought after personal development alternative available. As popular as Yoga and Starbucks! I want it to be sought after because of the consistent quality of the results clients receive from qualified practitioners, practitioners who understand their own strengths and areas of expertise and are constantly growing themselves in the world of horse and human potential.

As Alyssa Aubrey said, "You are in a collaborative. None of us know as much as we think we do. We are the gatekeepers to a sacred trust; we have to protect it."

You may decide you don't like me very much after we talk, for two reasons. One, if you're not ready to do this work, I'm going to tell you to go get some more training, hire a mentor, apprentice with a veteran of this work, and do your own deep inner work with the horses. Two, I'm going to tell you that building a sustainable practice takes real work over many years. It takes time and investment—emotional, mental, spiritual, physical, and financial investment.

If you've been doing your own work and are ready to begin (or start over), I can help you define your expertise, align with your ideal client, design a powerful program, and begin enrolling the clients you are most suited to serve at this time, immediately! But I cannot do the work for you. It takes consistent application, just like it took practice and application to learn to effectively facilitate meaningful change (Chris Irwin's words) for the human and the horse.

Choice Point

You can't cross the sea merely by standing and staring at the water.
—Rabindranath Tagore

We've come to the point where it's time to take action. You may have read this book straight through, nose to tail (sorry, couldn't resist) and plan to go back and work with the exercises later. Maybe you engaged with the exercises as you went along (or some of them). Maybe you actually applied some of the work to your own business. Here's the thing, unless you already have a background as a successful entrepreneur and marketer, the likelihood of you applying this information in a structured and consistent way is slim to none.

I had a conversation with a client recently, and we laughed at how often we know what to do, but if we're left alone to do it, it doesn't happen … we need structure, support, and accountability.

Before I wrote this book, I had done quite a bit of research on book coaches and publishing options. Then I came across Angela Lauria's book, *The Difference: 10 Steps to Writing a Book That Matters*. In the book, she laid out every single step I needed to take to get my book published, either on my own, through a traditional agent/publisher, or with her as a coach and publisher. I finished reading her book, looked over all of the steps required to publish my book on my own, and thought, *Yep, I could do all of this by myself.* And I knew in my bones it would never happen. I would spend months on the writing, get sucked into technical rabbit holes, and research my way into oblivion. I closed her book, went to her website, and filled out her application. 9-weeks later I had completed the first full draft of this book including all seven lessons. At the same time, I rebuilt my own training platform, enrolled 10 new clients, delivered numerous equine assisted trainings and workshops, and went on a 10-day vacation!

I share this with you because you are in the same place with your business that I was with writing this book. I understood the principles of what needed to happen, but there was no way I could make it happen by myself.

Again, unless you have a built-in following, or possess great entrepreneurial savvy and marketing experience, it is highly unlikely you will build a sustainable practice by yourself. Nor, should you have to! Working with a qualified mentor, coach, consultant in the building of your business will exponentially widen your community of support as well as enhance your own confidence, your ability to communicate, and, in Kathleen Barry Ingram's words, your ability to *hold the sacred space of possibility* for your clients.

Chapter Twelve

CONCLUSION

When we are motivated by goals that have deep meaning, by dreams that need completion, by pure love that needs expressing, then we truly live.
—Greg Anderson

At the beginning of this book, I introduced the 11 principles and attitudes that I believe are necessary to be prepared for a quantum leap into the next highest version of the grandest vision you have ever held for yourself. It is my sincere wish that you are significantly more prepared today than when we started this journey together!

Take a look at the principles again, and notice if the embodiment of them has deepened in any way.

The Principles and Attitudes of Quantum Leap Readiness

A Universal Lens: Are you able to see that your personal success means that you will be providing transformational experiences for hundreds and thousands of people over the lifespan of your career, and that will have a significant positive impact on the world?

Curiosity for Possibility: Do you now see the multitude of possibilities for you to share the wisdom of horses through your own super genius blend of who you are and what you do?

High Intention-Low Attachment: Can you set an audacious goal for yourself and not run for the hills the minute it looks like it's not working? It is always working.

Fierce Love: Are you able to love yourself as much as you love your family, horses, and clients? Can you stand in the power of *yes* and the liberation of *no*?

Trust: Can you trust the process and the evolution of your highest and best self? Can you trust that the Universe always conspires to serve you?

Acceptance: Do you accept what is happening in this moment as perfect, even if it's not what you want to be experiencing? And can you accept that you are the one to create a different experience?

Gratitude: Can you feel gratitude for what you have today as well as what you are about to receive even though you don't know where it's yet coming from?

Humor: Are you able to allow humor and amusement into the mundane aspects of building a business as well as the exceptional?

Discipline: Are you willing to commit to the work, the investment, and the rewards of building a profitable business?

Courage: Can you move forward even though you know the demons and closet monsters will roar and strike at the audacity of your bravery?

Reciprocal: Have you expanded your ability to receive in abundance as well as give great value?

Beggar No More

If your daily life seems poor, do not blame it;
blame yourself that you are not poet enough to call
forth its riches; for the Creator, there is no poverty.
—**Rainer Maria Rilke**

When I submitted my application to Angela Lauria at TheAuthorIncubator.com to be considered as an author client, one of the application questions was, "Why haven't you already written your book?" My response to that question was, "Because I have been learning and experiencing what needs to be shared." I have been becoming the person that has endured the evolution required to know what it takes to survive and then thrive as an entrepreneur in this budding new field of horses and personal development. And not just any entrepreneur, a soulful entrepreneur that wants a business built on integrity with win, win, win results for myself, my horses, and my clients!

I'm in my 10th year of this work, this life of constant internal expansion, exhilaration, and exhaustion. I see myself as a battle-worn pioneer that has finally come to the well of self-worth and can stand on my little pedestal and shout to the Heavens, "Who cares about the damn degree?! I know enough to make a difference right now!"

And guess what? So, do you!

Depending on where you were on your path when you started reading this book, you may have applied the lessons and are already enrolling new clients! Yay! Please send me a note, and let me know what is working best for you.

If you could use additional support navigating the process I have a fast-paced, fun, and effective program designed especially for you. I guarantee you will have a plan to enroll the clients you most want to serve before the end of the program and a design for steady, joyful income to feed your horses while you change the world!

Your time to make a difference is now. Your horse of opportunity is here, and it's time to ride. No matter what your false self has to say about it.

Oh, and by the way, remember I told you that on the journey to soulful entrepreneurship I smacked up against the biggest Aha of my life? I alluded to it in Chapter One when I shared, "After all of those years of inhaling the wisdom of the 'masters,' I was finally beginning to exhale. The work with the horses taught me to embody the wisdom in a way that was more than knowledge swirling around in my brain, it was now integrated into the next highest version of me. I felt like I was bestowed with new superpowers, and it was time to get to work saving the world!"

This is the secret formula to your horse and soul success....

It's Time to Exhale

You cannot continue to inhale information and hold it all in your brain without synthesizing it into practice and application. Do what you are ready to do now, and you will be qualified to do more, sooner than later!

Show Up. Be Yourself. Do Good Work. Love Your Clients. Receive. Give. Repeat!!!

CONTRIBUTIONS AND INSPIRATIONS

Alyssa Aubrey—www.CBEIP.org
Angela Dunning—http://www.thehorsestruth.co.uk/
Angela Lauria—www.TheAuthorIncubator.com
Chris Irwin—www.ChrisIrwin.com
Coherence Initiative—http://noosphere.princeton.edu/
Dr. Jenn Oikle—http://www.unitywithhorse.com
June Gunter—www.TeachingHorse.com
Kathleen Barry Ingram—www.sacredplaceofpossibility.com
Linda Kohanov—http://eponaquest.com/
Lisa Murrell—http://equinealchemy.com
Spring Forest Qigong—www.SpringForestQigong.com

Equine Assisted Coaching and/or Facilitation Training
CBEIP (.org)—Alyssa Aubrey
EAPD—Chris Irwin

Eponaquest—Linda Kohanov
Equine Guided Education—Arianna Strozzi Mazzucchi
Equus Coach Training—Koelle Simpson
Equine Alchemy—Lisa Murrell
Strides to Success—Debbie Anderson
The Academy of Coaching with Horses—Kathy Pike
Touched by a Horse—Melisa Pearce

Schelli's Reading (short and eclectic) List

Alyssa Aubrey / Jack Canfield—*The Road to Success* (moments of
awareness that lead to lasting change)

Angela Dunning—*The Horse Leads the Way: Honoring the True Role of
the Horse in Equine Facilitated Practice*

Dr. Bruce Lipton—*The Biology of Belief: Unleashing the Power of
Consciousness, Matter, and Miracles* (our thoughts have a biological
effect on our bodies)

Chris Irwin—*Horses Don't Lie* (making sense of the language of horse
in the life of a human)

Eric Butterworth—*Spiritual Economics* (spiritual principles and
abundance)

Jack Canfield—*The Success Principles: How to Get From Where You Are
to Where You Want to Be*

Jonathon Fields—*Uncertainty: Turning Fear and Doubt into Fuel for
Brilliance* (becoming an entrepreneur)

June Gunter—*TeachingHorse, Rediscovering Leadership* (personal and
professional leadership)

Kami Guildner—*Fire Dancer: Your Spiritual Journey to a Life of Passion
and Purpose*

Karla McLaren—*The Language of Emotions: What Your Feelings Are
Trying to Tell You* (emotions are Energy in Motion)

Linda Kohanov—*The Tao of Equus: A Woman's Journey of Healing and Transformation Through the Way of the Horse* (read everything she writes!)

Lynne Twist—*The Soul of Money: Transforming Your Relationship with Money and Life* (title speaks for itself)

Mark Rashid—*Nature in Horsemanship: Discovering Harmony Through Principles of Aikido* (mind, body and horsemanship)

Mike Dooley—*Leveraging the Universe: 7 Steps to Engaging Life's Magic* (a broader perspective on an abundant life)

Shannon Sikes Knapp—*Horse Sense, Business Sense: Hints and Hurdles to Starting Your Own Equine Assisted Program* (nuts and bolts business advice)

Dr. Tatiana Irvin—*The Reluctant Intuitive: A Soulful Confession and Practical Guide* (owning your innate gifts and powerful intuitive skills)

Tony Robbins—*Money, Master the Game: 7 Simple Steps to Financial Freedom* (what to do with your money as soon as you get some!)

ACKNOWLEDGEMENTS

I asked my Angels, "Who am I to write this book?" They said, "You are the sum total of all the ancestors that have poured their blood, sweat, and tears into this Earth; that have prayed and danced and birthed new life into your collective human consciousness. You are their voice that speaks today." Okay, no pressure there. Why did I ask? But ask I did. I have learned that if you ask, they will tell you. So be sure you really want to know the answer!

And so, I offer deep gratitude to all who have courageously laid their truth on the table, even in the face of ridicule. Thank you, dear Linda Kohanov, for your curiosity, diligence and incredible ability to take complex esoteric experiences and break them into digestible bites of extraordinary transformation. Thank God, the horse ancestors chose you to speak their truth!

Joe Whitehouse, husband, friend, champion. Your boundless patience, dedication, and crazy belief in me has been the most extraordinary lesson in unconditional love I have been blessed to experience. I love you too. And to our children, Anna and Grayson, who don't always understand me, but love me anyway and laugh at my jokes, even when I'm not very funny.

Thank you to my dad, Frank Barbaro for a curious mind that always wants to know—why, how, when, who, what is possible next? And God bless my mother, Sherry Barbaro who has helped to keep my feet on the ground so I don't completely float off the planet. I wouldn't have had the courage to write this book without your support and belief in me—no matter what. And to my dear, creative brother, Matthew Barbaro, who continually reminds me to 'wonder'.

Much, much, heartfelt gratitude to my mentors, friends and coaches that have helped to inspire, nurture, train, heal and feed my hungry soul. You are every bit a part of this book as I am. So, thank you to Carol Morrissey, Kathryn Riddle, and Ann Donaldson who knew me when, and love me still! To my karmic sister, Lisa Murrell and the whole Equine Alchemy herd for providing a most extraordinary container for learning and applying this life's work with horses. To dear, Maggie McGlynn, a most extraordinary facilitator and friend, thank you for teaching me to always see the highest and best in every human I meet. Thank you to June Gunter and Beth Hyjek who invited me into their circle of excellence and entrusted me with their sacred wisdom. And Dr. Tatiana Irvin, thank you for being a co-conspirator and friend and especially a master intuitive who truly helped to coach my soul out of hiding. Thank you, Nancy Rebecca, for helping me to banish the demons and learn to connect to and listen to my Higher Self. And Morgan Peterson, thank you for believing I have something important to teach, you inspire me! Thank you all for seeing the light in me, especially when I struggled to see it myself.

Thank you to all the amazing, courageous students and clients I have had the privilege to learn and co-create with. You have taught me the powerful impact of what it means to show up! A special shout out to those who were the first to jump into my new business program and are ready to *rock it!* Barb Haffner, Bobbi McIntyre, Deborah Pierce, Julie Georges, Julie Morton, Michelle and Randy Fetters, Nicole Parks, and Tracy Monthei-Smith. Nothing gives me greater joy than to celebrate your success!

And of course, buckets of carrots and apples for my herd of equine teachers and the horses all over the world that are patiently waiting for humans to simply live humanely. My Cruiser-doo is not only a Rock Star, he's my rock. Thank you to the human herd that cares for our beloved family of horses, Angie Taverna, Ashlee Melhado, Jeanne Melhado, Jessica Hudson, Liza, Sidney and Tammy Vinson, Morgan Peterson, and Wendy Christensen. And we couldn't run the place without the muscles, humor, love and support from Britt Vinson, David Melhado, Grayson Whitehouse and Joe Whitehouse. And finally, a special thanks to John and Christa McElveen of the Carolina Ear Research Institute for trusting us to care for their land and horses in service of a greater mission. It truly takes a village to make a positive difference.

I am over the moon with gratitude for the structure and support I've received from Angela Lauria and her team at the Author Incubator. Smart, creative, innovative, and fun. I thank my lucky stars you exist!

Big hugs to Maggie McReynolds, for her red pen and open heart. Especially the day I spent half my editing session crying on her shoulder after the loss of our dear horse coach, Petey. Maggie, you are a consummate space-holder and master of getting the work done anyway!

To the Morgan James Publishing team: Special thanks to David Hancock, CEO & Founder for believing in me and my message. To my Author Relations Manager, Margo Toulouse, thanks for making the process seamless and easy. Many more thanks to everyone else, but especially Jim Howard, Bethany Marshall, and Nickcole Watkins.

And to you Dear Reader, I whole-heartedly thank you for opening your soul to what is about to unfold....

About the Author

Schelli Whitehouse is a design expert for extraordinary equine inspired businesses. She helps equine assisted coaches, therapists, and facilitators weave their personal genius, ambitions, and philosophy into a lifestyle business with horsepower!

Her mission is to spread the power of equine inspired transformation and personal development by assisting other passionate practitioners to reach the people they are meant to serve.

Her combined experience as a professional actor, equine assisted coach, and business design consultant has given her an artistic approach and fluid connection to our human emotions.

Schelli is an Equine Alchemy Certified Coach and Facilitator. She has had the privilege to train and be mentored by master practitioners such as Lisa Murrell, founder of Equine Alchemy, Linda Kohanov, founder of Eponaquest and author of *The Tao of Equus* (among many other books). Maggie McGlynn, master leadership facilitator and founder of McGlynn Leadership, Inc. As well as June Gunter of TeachingHorse, an international equine experiential leadership program designed specifically for teams and corporate leaders.

In addition to her own coaching and business mentoring practice, Schelli hosts retreats for independent coaches and their exclusive clients.

Schelli lives in Raleigh, NC, with her husband and happy herd of horse coaches.

Website: www.SchelliWhitehouse.com

Facebook: www.facebook.com/EquineInspiredLife

THANK YOU

I appreciate you reading all the way to the end of this book!

If you are interested in joining a like-hearted group of equine assisted practitioners, check out my free Facebook group: "Love and Equine Assisted Prosperity".

We are supportive and inspiring each other to continue this great work! https://www.facebook.com/groups/LoveandEquineAssistedProsperity/

I'd love to know what you discovered about your own business from the reading and the lessons.

FREE ASSESSMENT and BUSINESS CLARITY SESSION: Want to chat about your own horse coaching program ideas and get my take? Complete the assessment and select a time to chat that works best for you: schelliwhitehouse.com/bch-assessment/

Sharing the passion...

To Your Horse & Soul Success,

—Schelli

Morgan James
Speakers Group

www.TheMorganJamesSpeakersGroup.com

We connect Morgan James published
authors with live and online events
and audiences who will benefit
from their expertise.

Morgan James makes all of our titles available
through the Library for All Charity Organization.

www.LibraryForAll.org